This book is dedicated to my
late father
Frederick <u>McMillan Morris</u>
my loving mother
<u>Flora Lockie Morris</u>
and all my family.

Copyright © 2005 Harry Morris.

Written & Compiled by Harry Morris.

Edited by Harry Morris.

Printed & Bound in Scotland by
Downie Allison Downie Bookbinders Ltd.

Front Cover Design by Morris & Davren.

Cover Photograph Courtesy of
Charles Margison.

'PC Archie Bauld
Created & Written by Harry Morris.

Illustrated by Derek Seal.

Additional Illustrations by Harry Morris.

ISBN 0-9549879-0-X

ISSN 1748 – 6106

Published in Scotland by Harry Morris.

Distributed by Harry Morris.

Harry Morris PO Box 7031
Glasgow. G44 3YN.

E.Mail : harry.morris51@virgin.net & info@harrythepolis.com

Website; www.harry-morris.com

Other titles available by Harry Morris;

'EVEN MORE LIES' : ISBN 09549879-1-8

FOREWORD

Harry Morris is a former Police Officer, who retired after performing 29 years Police Service.

He served with the City of Glasgow Police, Strathclyde Police, Scottish Police Forces.

During his illustrious and colourful career, he collated and wrote about many of the characters, incidents and humorous stories, he encountered in his time, with a view to someday, publishing a book about them.

This hilarious wealth of material from the various Law Courts, Beat Duties, Surveillance Operations, Football Details and everyday Policing in the Community, highlights a different perspective of our Serving Police Officers.

Enclosed is a compilation of Humorous Stories, Anecdotes, Jokes and Spontaneous Incidents referred to during his term of office within the Scottish Police Service.

He has also included some Cartoons of a colourful Police Character he created, P.C. ARCHIE BAULD.

INDEX

PART ONE

1) I'M JUST A MAN LIKE YOU.
2) GUNS IN THE FAMILY.
3) RAMBO.
4) SOMETHING MISSING.
5) HE'LL GO NUTS.
6) THE CANINE FAMILY.
7) CELL MATES.
8) THE TRUTH, THE WHOLE TRUTH.
9) WINDOW CLEANERS.
9) MORRIS'S SAFETY MOTTO.
10) THE HEILAN COO.
11) THE MIMIC.
12) IT'S YOURS.
13) POLICE ADVERT.
14) SHORT CUT.
15) FISHING FOR JAWS.
18) WHAT'S IN A NAME.
19) PEEK-A-BOO.
20) THE PACEMAKER.
21) NIGHT OUT, NOW AND AGAIN.
22) FRIENDS RE-UNITED.
22) SPEED CAMERA EXCUSE.

PART TWO

23) YE CANNY PARK THAT THERE!
26) ALL BETS ARE OFF!
27) ROAD ACCIDENT EXCUSES.
28) WEE POLIS.
29) B.A. WITH HONOURS.
30) DRUGS TRIAL.
32) NO COMPLAINTS.
33) BUDGIE AIRWAYS.
34) THE ADVENTURES OF PC ARCHIE BAULD.
35) ON THE BUSES.
43) CANTEEN PATTER.
44) GERMAN KNOCKERS.
45) IS THAT RIGHT?
45) ANOTHER VACANCY.

PART THREE

46) THE SMELL OF ROBBERY.
47) SPEEDING EXCUSE.
48) HELP THE AGED.
49) GRAFITTI.
50) DON'T CALL ME A LIAR.
51) PATON'S PLACE.
52) TV DETECTIVES.
54) THE GLASGOW SHERIFF COURT.
55) THE SHEEHY REPORT.
56) ILL-HEALTH RETIRAL.
56) THAT'S ENTERTAINMENT.
57) THE TASMANIAN DEVIL.
59) LEGLESS IN AUCHTERARDER.
60) FOOTBALL CRAZY.
61) FACE LIKE A FISH SUPPER, ALL CHIPS.
62) PIECES OF PIZZA.
62) TULLIALLAN BARBERS.
63) BRING BACK HANGING.
64) YOU SAID IT!
65) HOUSEBREAKING.
65) REDUCING CRIME.
66) NO CHANCE.

PART FOUR

67) DON'T TRUST THE POLIS.
67) HOW DID THEY KNOW?
68) JACKET IN!
70) CRUELTY TO GIRLFRIENDS.
71) THE CARBOLIC ALCOHOLIC.
74) I'M SICK! SICK! SICK! UP TO HERE.
75) MICHAEL SCHUMACHER – NOT!
76) VASECTOMY.
77) MOUSTACHE YOU A QUESTION.
78) TOILET GRAFITTI.
78) ROAD ACCIDENT EXCUSES.
79) TAXI TO CHARING CROSS.
81) THE SNITCH.

PART FIVE

82) A SPECIAL UNIT 'BURNS' SUPPER.
83) PEA AND HAM FROM A CHICKEN.
84) C.S.I. GLASGOW.
86) THE ADVENTURES OF PC ARCHIE BAULD.
87) A SIDE ORDER OF VEGETABLES.
88) EXAM RESULTS.
88) KICKING THE HABIT.
89) RED CARD FOR PINK SLIP.
90) ASK HIM YOURSELF.
91) TALKING SEX.
92) WHO'S COMFORTING WHO?
94) ROAD ACCIDENT EXCUSES.
94) POLICE PROVERB.
95) FORGOT WHO YOU WERE TODAY?
96) THE BAR – L STRIKE.
97) IS THAT A CANNON I HEAR?
98) TRAILER BIKE.
99) REMIND ME OF REMINSKY!

PART SIX

100) MARMALADE AND JAM.
101) KARAOKE? NOT!
101) ROAD ACCIDENT EXCUSES.
102) MINI A BARGAIN.
107) DON'T TALK TO STRANGERS.
107) ROAD ACCIDENT EXCUSES.
108) IN THE DARK.
108) WOOD U BELEEVE IT?
109) WHAT'S PERJURY?
109) ROAD ACCIDENT EXCUSES.
110) HELLO DOLLY.
111) DNA NOT REQUIRED.
112) CRIME DOESN'T ALWAYS PAY.
113) THE ADVENTURES OF PC ARCHIE BAULD.
114) WHO WAS THAT?
115) LOST FOR WORDS!
115) SMOKING COUGH!
116) THE JOB'S FUCKED.
117) NOW THAT'S MAGIC!

PART SEVEN

117) ROAD ACCIDENT EXCUSES.
118) WHO IS ABOOT?
118) CONTROL ROOM STORY.
119) STRAIGHT FROM THE HORSE.
120) KISS ME QUICK.
120) ROAD ACCIDENT EXCUSES.
121) THE BATTERY STORE.
122) I'LL TELL HIM TOMORROW, MAYBE!
125) A SECRET SERVICE.
126) WANTED.
127) LADIES AND GENTS, NO BOTHER.
127) BAD BREATH.
128) YUILL AND DODDS.
128) MONEY FOR OLD COKE.
129) SINGLE WHITE MALE.
130) NO PROFIT IN THEFT.
130) TOILET PAPER.
131) EVERYTHING IS FREE.
132) THREE IN A BED.
133) BARBERS.

PART EIGHT

133) CANTEEN.
134) FOOTBALL DETAIL.
135) LICENCED TO BLEED.
136) ROAST CHICKEN AND CHIPS.
140) COBBLERS.
141) FORENSIC PSYCHOLOGIST.
144) DR WHYTE AT YOUR DISPOSAL.
146) THE ADVENTURES OF PC ARCHIE BAULD.
147) SICK JOKE.
148) NO CHANGE.
150) SIGNING SESSION.
152) MAKE ME GO FASTER.
152) ROAD ACCIDENT EXCUSES.
153) DISPOSING OF EVIDENCE.
155) THE BALLAD OF BIG BAD ALEC.
156) NO HIDING PLACE.
157) NEW RELEASE.
157) MORE NEW RELEASES.

PART NINE

157) CREDIT FRAUD.
158) NO ARMCHAIR STAMPEDE.
159) CLASH OF PERSONALITIES!
160) DON'T BLOW A FUSE.
161) RELIGIOUS EXAMS.
161) LUCKY ME.
162) I NEVER PARKED IT LIKE THAT.
164) THE MUSIC OF LIFE.
165) LADIES AND GENTLEMEN BEN DOON.
167) HEARING THINGS.
168) HARRY THE UNKNOWN OSMOND.
169) GUESS WHO?
170) BOMBS AWAY.
171) TO HELL WITH TULLIALLAN.
172) FUNNY TEXT FROM A FRIEND.
172) GRASS IS GRASS.
173) ANTI ABORTION DEMO.

PART TEN

174) WHAT ARE YOU DOING?
175) THE COURT JESTER.
177) RELIEF FOR MY RELIEF.
178) THE SPARK-LE IS STILL THERE.
179) THE DEMOLITION MAN.
182) THE GLASGOW OLYMPICS.
183) LEARN TO DRIVE!
183) SPEED CAMERA EXCUSE.
184) THE ADVENTURES OF PC ARCHIE BAULD.
185) PARKING DISABILITY.
187) 0 – 60 IN SECONDS.
188) I'D KNOW HER ANYWHERE.
191) POST IT THRU' THE WINDOW.
193) THE LORD PROVOST OF RUSSIA.
194) REALITY TELEVISION.
195) SURPRISE! SURPRISE!
200) MY APPRECIATION.

'I'M JUST A MAN LIKE YOU'

This is a poem, which, to a lot of Police Officers in the service,
including myself, epitomises, what 'Policing' is all about.
I know for a fact, that many officers retain a copy
of it with them at all times, in the back
of their police issue notebook........
Read on and see why!

'I'M JUST A MAN LIKE YOU'

I have been where you fear to be
I have seen what you fear to see
I have done what you fear to do
All these things, I have done for you
I am the man you lean upon
The man you cast your scorn upon
The man you bring your troubles to
All these men, I have been to you
The man you ask to stand apart
The man you feel should have no heart
The man you call the man in blue
But I'm just a man, just like you
And through the years, I've come to see
That I'm not what you ask of me
So take these handcuffs and this baton
Will you take it? Will anyone?
And when you watch a person die
And hear a battered baby cry
Then do you think, that you can be
All these things that you ask of me?

Anon

'Guns in the Family'

One day a telephone call was received at the C.I.D. Office, from a male informant, who wished to remain anonymous.

The information was,
'There was several guns within the house at'...... and he supplied the young Detective Officer with the address.

The young Detective Officer, convinced that the call was genuine and keen to make a good impression, coupled with a discovery like this, arranged with other 'armed' C.I.D. Officers, to attend the house with a Warrant, to make a search of the premises for the alleged 'Firearms'!

As the C.I.D. Officers made their final preparations prior to leaving the Police Office, David Turner, an elderly bespeckled uniformed Officer, who was presently performing indoor duties, as the C.I.D. Office Clerk, overheard the entire episode of events and entered the room with his 'gold' rimmed half glasses perched on the bridge of his nose and carrying a copy of the public 'Voters Roll' log, for the entire area, under one arm.

Opening it up at a page he had previously marked off, he handed it over to the eager young Detective Officer and said,

"Aye son, your informant was spot on, there are 'Gunn's' at that address,

In fact, there's a whole family of them"!!

'Rambo'

During my probationer period in the Police, I worked in the Oatlands area of Glasgow, which bordered on the famous and notorious 'Gorbals'!

Whilst there, I worked with an old cop called 'Geordie Gunn', better known as Geordie Bang! Bang! He was, to put it mildly, 'completely aff his heid'! 'Puggled'! A 'total fruitcake'!

Now this was not only my opinion, this was the opinion of every officer on the shift, but, being fairly easy going and able to get on with most people, I decided to make my own mind up about him.

We had a few ups and downs during our working relationship, but nothing unduly worrying, that is, until our nightshift roster came around.

Now during the nightshift, part of your duties consisted of checking the security of shops and factories in your area.
As a pairing, one would check the front of the property and the other would check the rear. What you are looking for is 'break ins' or attempts.

However, if there were a line of shop properties, then you would check the front and rear yourself and do the properties alternatively.

One particular nightshift, about 04.00am in the morning, this was the procedure we had adopted, as we went along checking a line of shops.
I had gone to the rear of the property to check it and was coming back through to the front of the building.
As I did, I thought I heard something, so I slowly made my way out to the front of the building entrance and as I looked, there was

Geordie, with his back tight against the wall, peering in the next close-mouth entrance.

I thought he had seen or heard something, so I remained where I was, kept quiet and took observations.

As I watched Geordie from my nearby position, he then simulated taking a 'Hand Grenade' from his breast pocket and pulling out the imaginary 'safety pin', he then appeared as though he was throwing it into the property entrance.

Using perfect sound effects, he made the noise 'Boom'! As if it had exploded and then, giving the impression he was holding a 'Sub Machine Gun', he jumped in front of the tenement close entrance and began making a 'shooting' sound, 'Bang'! 'Bang'! 'Bang'! 'Bang'!

Only he was more realistic, that it sounded like the real thing exploding and a firearm being fired.

From then on I viewed Geordie, under a different light and was always very careful about coming out of any property entrance suddenly, just in case I surprised 'Geordie Bang! Bang!' and he mistook me for the enemy!! (And shot me with 'friendly' fire!)

'Something's Missing'!

While on Police patrol at a busy shopping centre, I was walking about, speaking with some of the 'shoppers', when I saw a 'buxom' young female coming toward me with one of her breasts blatantly exposed and hanging out of her blouse top for all to see.

I reacted immediately and took her to one side and asked her to explain this totally unsociable behaviour.

The young woman, stared at me for a moment, then a look of complete horror came over her face and as her eyebrows were raised, she blurted out in all sincerity,

"Shit! I've left my wean up in the canteen"!

'He'll Go Nuts'!

One refreshment period at work, one of the cops produced a bag of nuts from his food locker, which he added into his breakfast cereal.

"What kind of nuts are they"? I asked him.

"Almonds"! He replied. "The wife was given them as a present, from one of the old men she looks after".

Now, to let you understand, this particular cops wife worked as a 'Care Assistant' to the elderly and made regular visitations to their homes.

However, with this in mind, I had an occasion to speak with his wife at a Police Function.
During the conversation, I was saying to her about the 'almonds' and I suggested, she talk the elderly man into buying 'walnuts' and give them to me, for a change.
She appeared to blush slightly, then said,

"Do you know the full story, behind the almonds"?

Unaware of what she was talking about, I shook my head.

She then confided in me, (I love it!) and related the following story, which she made me swear, I'd keep to myself!

Apparently, while visiting one of her elderly patients, he had asked her if she liked 'almond' nuts.

She stated she didn't, but her husband was very fond of them.

At that, the elderly patient presented her with a glass jar, full to the brim with 'almonds', to give to her husband.

Delighted by the old man's kind gesture, the cop had 'tucked' into them, munching them while watching TV, eating them in his breakfast cereal, adding them to his Indian 'curry', in fact, anything you could add nuts too, etc.

The following week, on returning to the elderly patient on her routine visit, she handed him a large 'Galaxy' chocolate bar as a thank you for the almonds.

The old man thanked her kindly and producing a full jar of 'Sugar Almonds', he said,

"I'll give you this jar as well, once I have 'sooked' all the sugar icing off them"!!

Yuck!!

'The Canine Family'

On attending the report of vandalism to an elderly couples home, I was informed that a neighbour's ten years old son, had entered their private garden and pulled out some of their flowers.
He then proceeded to scatter them about the grass lawn and pathways.

I asked the elderly couple if they had spoken with the parents of the boy regarding his behaviour?

The elderly woman replied,

"No way, the father's a boxer"!

Quick as a flash the elderly male retorted,

"Aye"! "And the mother's a bit of a dog as well"!!

'Cell Mates'

Whilst working for a short time with the Courts Staff Branch, I was detailed along with an elderly Police Colleague, to form part of the police escort on the 'Prison Bus' as it made it's way around the various courts uplifting the convicted prisoners bound for Her Majesty's Prison 'Barlinnie' or 'Bar-L' as it was better known.

While performing this duty, an arrogant male prisoner, who had just received a very long custodial sentence, was trying to give the impression that he was a 'Hard Man' to the other prisoners on the bus.

This he did by verbally mouthing off at my colleague and I, in a derogatory fashion, using foul and abusive language.
This action received a minimum response of laughter from the other jail bound passengers, most of whom were deep in thought.

At this point, my elderly colleague, who was the 'butt' of most of his remarks, leaned over him and said, in a very calm and assured voice,

"You have a good laugh while you can son, because see tonight when I'm sharing my comfortable warm double bed with my lovely wife Mary, you unfortunately my son, will be sharing your hard single bunk bed with a 19 stone, tattooed, homosexual, skinhead called 'Shuggie'!"

Along with the rest of the jail bound passengers, he had to laugh, but it was an obvious nervous laugh,

That I almost felt sorry for him!!!! **NOT!**

'The Truth, The Whole Truth'

A young newly appointed Police Officer was cited to attend court for the first time in order to give evidence for the prosecution in a trial involving a 'Breach of the Peace'.

During his evidence, the young officer stated that the accused had been bawling, shouting, cursing and swearing in a public place.

The Procurator Fiscal asked the young officer to tell the court what they had actually shouted during the disturbance.

The young cop replied,

"They were shouting that the police were a bunch of 'Effen Bees' sir"!

"Yes Constable, I appreciate what you are saying and realise that you are trying to spare our blushes, but I need you to tell the court the exact words they used"? Explained the Fiscal.

"They swore at us sir"! Said the young cop.

"Yes we know that Constable, but what I want you to tell the court today is the actual words the accused used when they swore at you"?

Explained the Procurator Fiscal, who was by now becoming exasperated by the inexperience of his young police witness.

"They shouted that we were a bunch of 'Fucken Bastards' sir".

Blurted out the young cop.

"Thank you for that"! Replied the relieved Fiscal before continuing.

"And did you apprehend them"? He then asked.

To which the young cop replied without any hesitation,

"You're Fucken right we did"!!

'Window Cleaners'

A female telephoned the police office and reported,

"Somebody has just poured 'yoghurt' or 'cream' all over my bedroom window"!

I said to the female,

"Well, can you not just go out and clean it off"?

The rather perturbed female replied,

"What"!! "With a disabled son"?

At which point I paused for a moment, before answering,

"I think that's a bit drastic missus, I was going to suggest that you use water"!!

'Morris's Safety Motto'

'Feel secure at night, sleep with a Policeman'!

'The Heilan Coo'

A few years ago, back in the days of the City of Glasgow Police Force. A newly promoted, young and ambitious Inspector arrived at the Gorbals Police Office, on a 'whim', like the proverbial 'new broom'.

One day, he called in the older and more experienced Sergeant into his office.

"Willie", he said, "Have you ever heard of a female from the Govanhill area of Glasgow, nick-named the 'Heilan Coo'?

The elderly Sergeant thought for a moment, shook his head and said,

"Can't say I have". "Why"? "Should I"?

"Well", said the Inspector,

"I have it on good authority that this female is 'allegedly', allowing Police Officers into her house to drink alcohol and sample her 'sexual' favours!

"Och, I don't believe that for a minute". Replied the Sergeant rather dismissively.

"Well that's what I've heard". Said the Inspector. "But we'll see"!

A few weeks later, the Inspector received more information, which was relative to the enquiry he was making and this time there was an address to go with it.

He rushed into the Sergeants room.

"Quick Willie, come with me, I've got an address to check out. I think it could be the house belonging to the Heilan Coo".

Both Supervisors left the office and made their way down the road on foot.

Finally, they arrive at the address.
It's a large red sandstone tenement building in the Govanhill area of Glasgow.
Confirming the address with his notebook, he said, "This is it"!

He appears very excited by this news and as they enter the close mouth entrance, he said, "It's on the first landing to the right Willie".

They approach and knock on the door.

There's a moment or two passes, before the door is eventually opened by a small 'dirty faced' little boy, who on seeing the Police Officers standing there, stood staring back at them.

Then a female voice, with a 'South Uist' accent, called out from inside the house. "Well, who is it William"?

To which the small boy replied, "It's Uncle Willie, wi' another wan o' his pals"!!!

'The Mimic'

One day while out driving with my 4 years old daughter Samantha in the rear seat, a Van driver, came racing up on my off-side and swerved in front of me, causing me to take evasive action to prevent a collision.
Receiving such a fright and forgetting for a moment about my young passenger in the rear seat, I reacted by shouting out at him, "Away ya stupid Bastard"!

Suddenly, I received a sharp reminder of her presence, when she uttered, loud and clear from the back seat,

"Daddy! Don't call the man a stupid bastard"!

'It's Yours'

One day whilst working away in the front of the Police Office, the door opened and in came two little 'twin' girls, with hair in 'pig tails' and carrying a small puppy dog.

"Hello there"! I said. "And whose wee dog is this then"?

Both girls answered in unison, "It's weers"!

"We don't say, it's 'weers', we say, it's ours"! I replied.

"But it isn't yours". Responded both girls. "It's weers"!

"Yes I know that". I said, pausing for a moment before continuing.

"But if you both own something, then what we would say is, it's ours"!

Both girls looked at me rather unconvincingly, but said, "Okay then"!

"Right now, let's start again. Whose is the wee dog"? I asked them again.

Both girls looked at each other for a moment, then replied in unison,

"It's yours"!!

R.U. FEELING EXHAUSTED KNACKERED SUICIDAL DEPRESSED SHOCKED AND TOTALLY SCUNNERED?

THEN THERE'S A CAREER FOR YOU WITH

THE POLICE!

'Short Cut'

A group of workmen arrived at a certain Police Office in Pollokshaws, to install a complete new Central Heating System.

All day, they beavered away, ripping out the old heating system and installing the new 'slimline' 'white' radiators to the wall.

Next, they measured up and cut all the required copper piping to the exact sizes, in preparation for the following day when they returned, then all that was needed, was for them to connect the pipes to the new 'central heating' radiators ..... 'Wrong'!

During the previous night, some of the Officers on nightshift decided to try out the fancy little pipe cutting machine, which the workmen had neglected to put away and had stupidly left out.

One at a time, each Officer had a go at cutting an inch off all the copper pipes left lying around the office ...... Great fun!

However, next day there was total confusion within the office as the workmen tried to fit the meticulously measured cut pipes, only to discover they were all an exact inch short!

Needless to say, nobody in the Police Office put them wise as to how such an error could possibly have been made by professional workmen.

As for all the cut pieces of copper piping, well allegedly they were discarded in the River Clyde sometime during the night, when one of the suspect 'Police Plumbers' realised the extent of what they had done!

'Fishing for Jaws'

While a student at the Police College, Tulliallan, the pride of place was a 'fantastic' six feet Tropical Fish Tank, with a wide variety of small 'shoals' of many different shapes, sizes and extremely colourful specimens.

This wonderful focal point of attention, took centre stage, in the main entrance of the College 'Crush Hall', for all to see.

At that time, my father was also a keen enthusiast for keeping Tropical Fish and I was informing the College Sergeant of this, who had accepted the responsibility of looking after the maintenance of the tank and was feeding the fish.

"Well, if he ever has an abundance of fish, tell him I'll accept any surplus he has for our Aquarium"! He said.

With this in mind, the following weekend, whilst visiting my parents, I was telling my father about the College Aquarium and the request for any surplus fish for their impressive tank.
As it was, he did have some surplus fish and supplied me with three large tropical species called 'Oscars'!

Packed safely in a double layer of polythene bags and wrapped in towels to keep the heat in, I made my way back to the Police College the following Sunday evening.

On my arrival, I immediately went to the Police Instructors Office, looking for Sergeant Lancaster, in order to present him with the 'Oscars', to add to his impressive array of tropical fish.
However, I was informed he would not return to the College, until the following morning.

Armed with my bag of 'Oscars', I went to the 'Crush Hall' and opening the tank hood, I placed the bag in the aquarium water, in order to acclimatize the 'Oscars' to their new surroundings.

Later the same evening, before I retired to my dormitory for the night, I returned to the aquarium and opening the bags, I introduced the 'Oscars' into their new abode.

I watched for several minutes, as the new arrivals swam around the aquarium, surveying every inch of their new home, as they settled in.

Next morning, I arose and headed down to the dining hall for my breakfast convinced that my contribution had earned me some much needed 'Brownie' points at the Police College and they would be a good addition and a pleasant surprise for the entire staff.

En-route, I met Sergeant Lancaster in the corridor as he was arriving and briefly informed him of my new introductions to his 'show piece' tropical fish aquarium.

"Great stuff Morris"! He said. "I'll check them out later"!

A short time later, halfway through my 'Cornflakes' and 'Kippers', I swear the College building shook, as a voice screamed out,

"MORRIS"! "Where are you"?

Not the cheery voice I expected to hear. I looked over towards the door, to see a very irate Sergeant Lancaster enter the dining room with 'steam' blowing out of his ears.
'Lancaster' by name and 'Lancaster' by nature! This guy was flying!

What was wrong? I asked myself.

Apparently, the new arrivals to his prized aquarium, which I had introduced ..... had massacred and subsequently eaten most of his aquatic fish stock during the night and what they didn't eat, they maimed or killed for later, leaving the tank resembling a scene from the 'Amity' beach resort in the film 'JAWS'!

Which reminds me of a quick joke.

How did they know that the girl in 'JAWS' had dandruff?
Because, she left her 'Head and Shoulders' on the beach!

(Okay! Okay! It was funny at the time.)

Anyway, there were wee bits of 'fishy' heads, tails, parts of fins and bodies discarded everywhere, floating about the tank.

"What the hell did you put in my beautiful aquarium, it looks like it has been blown up"?

He enquired, trying to curb his obvious anger, as his 'pride and joy' showpiece and main foyer focal point, was reduced to what could only be described as a 'battlefield'.

As I stood there, trying to summon up an acceptable answer, my nerves got the better of me and I couldn't prevent myself from laughing hysterically, as I watched one of my 'fishy' friends, swimming effortlessly past, with a large 'Angel' fish dangling out of the side of it's mouth.

As for Sergeant Lancaster, he didn't see the funny side and stormed off to his office. The alternative action would have been to 'batter' me or give me a right good 'dressing' down, I think!

For the rest of my time at the College, I had to maintain a very low profile when around him.
I also had to endure the endless jokes,

"Hey Morris, I've got an aquarium at home, can you 'Fillet'?

"Good 'Cod' Morris, there's something 'Fishy' about you"! And my particular favourite,

"Hey Harry, I heard you went out with a 'Mermaid' to a 'crustacean' disco and pulled a 'Mussel'!

With regards to the trio of 'Oscar' fish, well, suffice to say, they went on to clean up and lived happily ever after, in the showpiece aquarium, within the Crush Hall at the Police College, in Tulliallan.

They also continued to grow very big on their 'Seafood' diet.

With my intervention and influence, it became a much more safer 'Plaice'!

However, I'm reliably informed that since I've left, the Tulliallan Police College,

'Fins' just ain't what they used to be!

'What's in a Name'

As a uniformed officer, I was walking along the corridors of Police Headquarters, when I saw, approaching me from the opposite direction, an old colleague, who had been recently promoted to Chief Inspector.

This was an old friend, with whom I had joined the City of Glasgow force and had worked with, when we were both Probationary Constables.

As we got closer, I put my hand out to greet him and said,

"Hello Ricky, how are you doing"?

Slightly embarrassed by my greeting, he looked around to check if anyone had heard me and said,

"If you don't mind Harry, don't call me Ricky"!

Disgusted by this reaction, I retorted,

"Why"? "Have you changed your name"?

'Peek – a – Boo'!

Big Alex Morgan was a colleague of mine from our days in the Traffic Department and he had two young daughters.

One of his daughters, Suzanne, who was about three years old at the time, was going through a phase where she would lift up her Mums dress or skirt and try and look under.
(Obviously been watching her dad Alex)!

Anyway, one particular day, while Alex was out with Suzanne, he was travelling on a Public Transport Bus, where there was 'Standing Room Only'!

While standing there with one hand holding Suzanne and the other holding the passenger rail, Suzanne decided to have a look under the female passenger's skirt, standing next to them, facing the opposite way.

Just as she lifted the woman's skirt up, Alex looked down and saw her and pulled her hand away from the woman's skirt, taking her to the other side of him, but as he did so, the woman's skirt creased and stayed up at the back, so Alex, being a gentleman, tried to right the wrong doing of his daughter and bent over behind the woman.
He then, ever so gently, tried to turn her skirt hem back down.

However, just as he bent over his 6' feet 4" inches of 'gangly' body to do so, the woman, obviously felt something, turned around and caught him in the uncompromising position of touching her skirt.

The woman stared down at Alex in his present position and gave a look of utter disgust at his behaviour.

As for Alex?

Well, red faced and totally embarrassed about the entire episode of events, he tried in vain to explain and convey apologies for his daughter's behaviour, but having looked at Suzanne's angelic and innocent little face, I doubt very much if the woman ever believed him!

'The Pacemaker'

Mrs Brown was the mother in law of my brother Allan and stayed with him and his wife Mary for many, many years.

She had been a healthy woman for most of her life, but several years before she died, she was beginning to experience tiredness and breathing problems.
Her sons and daughters convinced her she would have to go and see the Doctor and a consultation was duly arranged.

After the Doctors examination, it was his diagnosis that Mrs Brown required an operation to have a 'Pacemaker' fitted.
This did not auger well with the 92 years old Mrs Brown, who had only ever been in a hospital, when visiting family or friends.

Her son Willie sat down with her one day and explained that it wasn't a 'major' operation anymore and many people had the operation performed and were enjoying a much healthier lifestyle.
She sat digesting all the 'pros' for having such an operation done and asked Willie,

"And how long will this 'pacemaker' thing last, after it's fitted"?

"It'll last at least fifteen years Mum"! Replied an excited Willie.

She paused for a moment before blurting out in all sincerity,

"A knew it! That would mean I'd need to go back in and have it done all over again"!

'Night Out, Now and Again'

I worked with big David Turner, who when off duty, became a good friend of mine and we would socialise regularly.

One night, David and his wife were over at my house for a meal and a few drinks.
During the evening, my kids had joined us, prior to going to bed and Samantha, my eldest daughter, decided to ask,

"Uncle David, do you drink every night"?

"Don't be silly darling, apart from I couldn't afford it, your Aunt Margaret wouldn't allow me"! David replied.

"Well, how often do you drink then"? She asked him.

"Let me think"! Said David, rubbing his chin.

"On a Monday, I go to the Police Club to play Darts ….. and I'll maybe have 2 or 3 pints… Just to steady the nerves.

Then on Tuesday, I play Billiards at the British Legion Club and I'll have a couple of pints of Guinness. It's good in there…

Wednesday, I'll go to the Football and maybe have 1 or 2 pints… to celebrate or commiserate the result of the game….

Thursday's, I'll stay in with your Aunt Margaret and relax with a few Gin and Tonics ……

Friday, now that's my Snooker Club night. So I'll go for a pint or two afterwards …..

Saturday is my day at the Horse Racing, so I'll usually have a bet on a few horses and afterwards, win or lose, I'll have a right good 'bevy' of 'Gin' and Tonics, washed down with a few beers.....

Then, finally on Sunday, I usually sit in with a 'carry out' and watch the highlights of the Rugby on television!

So, the answer to your question Samantha, is probably 'Yes'!

But in saying that,

You would have to agree, I do like my Sport!!

'Friends Re-united'

I was asked recently if I had ever gone 'on-line' and visited the website titled 'Friends Re-united', to find out the whereabouts and maybe recognise and correspond with some of my old school friends.

I responded by saying I had no need to visit the site, as I worked in 'Crime Intelligence' and had first hand knowledge of where most of them were!

'Speed Camera Excuses'

'I was en-route to my nephews wedding and was being followed to the church by a friend, the 'Official Wedding Photographer'.

As we were running slightly late, I saw the 'flash' and I just assumed it was just him trying out his Camera Flash, in order to be prepared to start photographing the bride and groom on his arrival.

Therefore, I refute any allegation that I was speeding'

'Ye Canny Park That There'!

Working with the City of Glasgow Police, I met and got to know many true characters, none more so than 'Big Willie Irvine'.
Willie was a 'big man' in every sense of the word and lived in the 'Bridgeton' area of Glasgow, where a 'Square Go' was a semi-organized, bare knuckle fistfight between two men, without the use of weapons.

Now this was unfair, because Big Willie had hands like 'shovels' and was built like a 'brick shit-house' and with these attributes, it is safe to say, he didn't have a lot of enemies, mind you, those who were, he just 'battered'!

Suffice to say, most of the people who knew him, decided it was better to be regarded as his friend and keep him on your side!

One afternoon, while out on a 'drinking binge' or 'pub crawl' as they say in Glasgow, Willie found himself in the wrong area, as the 'Demon' drink took it's toll and he found himself in the old 'Dalriada' Hotel, in Edinburgh Road, Glasgow.

Unaware of Willie's reputation and to a certain extent, slightly blind as to his physic, some of the local 'young bucks', having downed a pint of the local 'Snakebite', (cloudy lager) and had 'sniffed' the barmaid's apron, to top up their own individual 'bravado', they began to throw their weight about, amongst the assembled drinkers in the pub, including Willie and even had the audacity to direct some verbal abuse his way.

Not a man to take this lying down, Willie responded with his own brand of retaliatory verbal abuse, but the young bucks, became one too many for him to challenge, (they numbered nine or ten in all).

Outnumbered, even for the physical presence and reputation of Willie, he left the pub under a barrage of abusive verbal remarks.

However, retreat, is not a word you'll find in Willie's limited vocabulary and he was not about to let it drop!

A short time later, Willie appeared at his brother's house, asking to borrow his car.
He gave the excuse of having an errand to run.

Willie's brother relented under his constant persuasive pressure and reluctantly handed Willie the keys to his car!

'Armed', with a motor vehicle and I use that word literally, Willie drove off.

Several minutes of continuous driving, Willie turned onto Edinburgh Road and made his way along, towards the 'Dalriada' Hotel.

Almost parallel with the 'Dalriada' entrance, Willie turned sharp left onto the footpath, straight across the 'grassed' area in front of the Hotel and accelerated, driving his brothers motor vehicle, straight through the double door entrance of the Public Bar, sending tables, chairs, drinks, 'punters' and debris, sprawling helplessly across the floor.

Others in the bar area, ran for cover, as their eyes 'popped' in total shock and disbelief, at the impact and destruction created by Willie's actions.

However, unfortunately for Willie, as he tried to exit the motor vehicle in order to 'reek' more physical damage on the 'patrons' of the 'Dalriada Hotel, he found the car doors were wedged in the doorway entrance, making it impossible, even for Willie to open them.

As he huffed and puffed, trying repeatedly to get out, it became obvious to the fleeing patrons, that he was stuck and they quickly rounded on the car, like a hungry pack of wolves.

As they pounded 'bar stools' and 'broken chairs' on the laminated windscreen, trying to gain entry to Willie, he was inside, kicking the rear window of the car out, in an attempt to make good his escape.

Just as Willie hauled his large frame through the space and crawled out across the boot lid of the car, he was 'rescued' and promptly arrested by the local Police, who were responding to an emergency call, reporting the entire incident.

Willie's unbelievable 'Evel Knievel' stunt, had prompted a quicker than usual response from the local 'cops', all wanting to see this for themselves!

Whether Willie was fortunate of the Police presence, or the local 'young bucks' were saved the ultimate embarrassment of being beaten to a pulp, by a Glasgow 'Hard Man' with a reputation to back it up, we'll never know.
I have my own opinion of what the outcome would be!

Subsequently, Big Willie expected and received a custodial sentence for his reckless actions, but I can still remember him saying to me,

"If you can't do the time, then don't do the Crime"!

I personally think, that is sound advice to anybody thinking about a career in Crime!

What a pity we could not employ Big Willie to enforce it!

'All Bets Are Off'!

'Tank', the likeable rogue from the Bridgeton area of Glasgow, received some unexpected bad news, when visiting the Cardiology' Department of the Royal Infirmary, for a check up.

It appeared, he required immediate 'Triple Heart Bypass Surgery' and the Doctor wanted him admitted, the following day.

'Tank', informed some of his friends regarding his news and the following scenario, is the reaction he received from his old 'Bridgeton' buddies.

"Can I get your car"? "Seeing that you'll probably die during the operation"! Remarked Wee Dougie.

"Naw I won't"! Replied a confident Tank.

"Ye might, it's a big operation that". Came back Dougie.

"Nay chance"! Said Tank. "I'm as strong as a hoarse"!

"Right then"! Said Dougie. "I'll bet you, ye die in the theatre"!

"I'll bet ye I frigging don't"! Replied Tank.

"Right, yer on. How much"? Enquires Dougie.

"I'll bet ye a 'Tenner'! Said Tank. (That's £10.00 in money)

They both lick their thumbs and rub them together sealing the £10.00 bet.

A couple of days later, Tank is admitted into Hospital and underwent his Triple Bypass Operation.
Afterwards, he is wheeled out into 'recovery' before being admitted to the Intensive Care Unit for observations.

Wee Dougie, on hearing that Tank has gone through his operation, contacted Tank's wife and enquired how he is and can he visit him in Hospital?

He is informed the operation has gone well and that Tank is in the I.C.U. but they are only allowing visiting for close family members only.

Wee Dougie is concerned about his good friend and decides to 'con' his way in the ward, to pay Tank a visit.

As he arrives at the I.C.U. he informs the nursing staff that he is there to visit his 'brother' Tank and is directed down to the far end of the ward, where Tank is situated.

Dougie, slightly apprehensive as to how is old friend will be, begins his slow walk down the ward towards Tank.

As he gets closer to the bed, he can see several metal stands and bright monitors around him, with various tubes leading from them, going into Tank's body and he is lying with his head to one side and his eyes closed, apparently asleep.

On seeing all this highly technical monitoring equipment, he nervously bent over the hospital bed to look at Tank's face and as he does, Tank opened one eye, looked straight at Dougie's face, put his hand out in front of him and said with total conviction,

"TENNER"!!

'Road Accident Excuses'

'I had been shopping for house plants all day and was on my way home.
As I approached the intersection, a large hedgerow sprang up, obscuring my vision and I collided with another car, which I did not see'!

'Wee Polis'

One evening, the Police received an urgent call for assistance from an elderly female who sounded distressed.
The Police Officers, led by the new shift Inspector, immediately made their way to the location.
On arrival at the locus, they knocked on the door of the house and a female voice enquired from inside,

"Who is it"?

"It's the Police"! Replied the Inspector.

"Who"? Responded the elderly female.

"It's the Police m'dear, can you open the door and let us in"? He replied.

"How do I know you're the Polis"? The female enquired.

"I can assure you m'dear, I am the Police"! He said.

"Is that right"? "Well, how do I know"? Said the female in response.

"Well"! Said the Inspector, beginning to lose his patience.
"You could look through your letterbox and you'll see I'm a Police Officer"!

At that, the Inspector, who is (6' 2") six feet and two inches in height, knelt down on the floor landing and opened the elderly females letterbox, for her to see out.

The elderly woman looked out at the Police Officers face, looking back at her.

At this response, the Inspector, then points to his 'cap badge' and the 'braiding' on his hat and said,

"See, I told you, I'm the Police"!

The elderly female stared for a moment, then responded,

"Away you tae hell! You're too wee for a Polis"!

'B.A. with Honours'

A young career minded Police Officer, was selected to participate on the force accelerated promotion scheme, to become a Sergeant.
He was informed he would be moved around the various offices and departments for experience.
The following day, the officer concerned, was sent to work at the Divisional Headquarters for a few weeks.

On his first day, he was instructed by the Senior Sergeant, to make his way around the entire headquarters building and perform an inventory, on how many fire extinguishers there were and their exact locations.

The young Sergeant, slightly bemused by this request, said,

"With all due respect Sergeant, do you mean to tell me that I, a person who studied five years at Caledonian University to attain a B.A. with Honours, in order that my first assignment as a newly promoted Sergeant, would be, to try and find my way around an office, which I've never worked in before and note down how many fire extinguishers there are and their exact location"?

The senior Sergeant looked at him and said, "What did you get the Degree for"?

"Geography"! Replied the young Sergeant indignantly.

"Good"! Said the Senior Sergeant, "You won't get lost then, will you"?

'Drugs Trial'

At a recent 'Drug Dealers' trial within the High Court in Glasgow, a uniformed Police Officer was explaining to the assembled jury, why he was involved in the 'Raid' with undercover Drug Squad Officers and his 'role', in the subsequent search of the suspect's property.

As a result of his actions, a large amount of 'Drugs' were recovered and three persons arrested and charged, in connection with it.

The Defence QC for the main accused asked the Police Officer, to explain again, his part in the 'Operation' and subsequent search for Drugs.

The Officer stated, on gaining entry to the house, along with the 'Drug Squad' Officers, they began a meticulous search, one room at a time.

It was whilst engaged in this search he observed the main accused, acting very suspiciously on one of the beds within the room.

The Officer stated, he moved him off the bed and lifted the mattress, to reveal a 'bag' containing a quantity of 'Drugs'!

At this point, the Defence QC interrupted and asked,

"How did you know it was 'Drugs' in the bag"?

The Officer replied,

"It was a clear plastic bag and I could see the 'Drugs' inside, they were in tablet form"!

The Defence QC then said,

"So you could tell immediately they were 'Drugs', is that right"?

"Yes sir"! Replied the Officer.

The Defence QC then said,

"I would like for you to answer 'Yes' or 'No' to the following questions".

He then picked up a 'clipboard' and pen from his table and asked the Officer,

"Are you a Chemist"?

"No"! Replied the Officer.

The Defence QC appeared to write something down on the clipboard, before continuing.

"Are you a Pharmacist"?

"No"! Repeated the Officer.

The QC appeared to write down something again.

"Are you an Alchemist"?

"No"! Replied the Officer for a third time.

"Well", began the Defence QC, "Could you please explain to the Ladies and Gentlemen of the Jury, how you can stand there and say that you knew they were 'Drugs', just by looking at them"?

The Defence QC then raised his eyebrows, cocked his head to one side and stared at the Police Officer, inviting an answer.

The Officer paused for a moment, as if to give his experienced questioner a ray of hope.

He then, 'rapped' his knuckle off the wooden witness podium and said,

"Same as I can tell you this is made of wood, but I'm not a 'Joiner'!!

Suffice to say, the Jury fell about laughing and the Defence had lost a vital point!

'No Complaints'

A young female Police Officer was attending an 'Officer Safety Training Course', within the Police Training Centre.

During the events of the day, she was paired off with an Inspector, in order to demonstrate her self - defence moves.

Whilst engaged in this part of the exercise, the Inspector, accidentally struck her on the head, with a 'plastic' training baton, whereby, the Policewoman sustained a slight bruise to her head.

After receiving some First Aid to her injury, she was able to continue with her training course.

Several days later, the same Inspector was engaged in the front office of a crowded Police Station, when the same Policewoman entered.

Immediately, on recognising her from the 'Officer Safety Training Course', the Inspector enquired across the crowded office,

"How is your head Angela"?

To which the Policewoman shouted back,

"Well, I've never had any complaints so far"!

'Budgie Airways'

Whilst a member of Strathclyde Police Motorcycle Section, there was an older Officer in particular, who claimed to have been a veteran of the **R.A.F. (Royal Air Force).**

I would continually 'rib' him and 'wind' him up and refer to the **R.A.F.** he was in, as being **RUDE, ARROGANT** and **FLY.**

One particular day, we were within the Motorcycle Section Canteen having our lunch and I was deliberately 'ribbing' Old Harry, as usual.

"Come on Harry, tell me what Aircraft you have flown yourself"? I asked sarcastically.

I continued by asking, "The Concorde, a 747, the Starship Enterprise"?

As quick as a flash, in his droll, dry sense of humour, Harry replied,

'U.F.O.'

To this day, I'm not sure if he was just exaggerating, or telling me where to go!!

Moody bugger!

"THE ADVENTURES OF PC ARCHiE BAULD"

BY 'SEAMOR TOONS'

'On the Buses'!

Several years ago, whilst still a serving Police Officer, my younger brother Hughie was a Corporation Passenger Transport Driver.
In layman's terms, he drove a big orange and green double deck bus about the housing schemes of Glasgow, picking up and dropping off passengers.

It was the practice of all drivers employed on the buses, to save money throughout the year and hold a Special Sports Night Competition, with free alcohol and buffet for all involved.

They would acquire a local Social club and make the necessary arrangements for their 'Free' night of entertainment with monetary rewards, along with trophies for the winners.

Through my younger brother Hughie, I got to know a lot of the drivers and on these Special occasions, I would receive an invitation to come along and join in.

It was 7 pm on the Friday night when Hughie arrived to pick me up in a taxi.
He was wearing a white suit and tee shirt to match, in total contrast to me, who was wearing a black suit and black tee shirt. Making me appear like a photographic negative of him.

"Change your suit Hughie"? I asked him.

"No way"! He said. "I look like 'Brian Ferry' in this suit"!

"I don't know about Brian, but you definitely look like a 'Fairy' that's for sure". I remarked.

Anyway, Hughie was not for changing his new look, so off we went on our night out looking like the new 'Randall and Hopkirk' Deceased!

On our arrival, the Committee Members who ran the entire event, would hand out raffle tickets, five at a time, to the assembled member drivers.

Each raffle ticket handed over at the bar, was the equivalent of one drink, therefore, five raffle tickets equalled five pints of heavy / lager or any spirit you cared to order.

As the Committee Member carried out the distribution of tickets, (by the way, every fifteen minutes), he would say to me,

"Sorry Harry, but Hughie will have to share his drink raffles tickets with you"!

Then as he was about to move away, he would turn back and as subtle as a 'brick to the head', would press ten raffle tickets into my hand.
This would annoy Hughie, who would say,

"How come he gave you more 'drink' tickets than me"?

"What's the difference"? I said, "We're both going to drink them"!

"Aye, right enough. I'll go and get them. Is it Rum and Coke for sir, with a beer chaser, or are you on the Whisky tonight"?

"One thinks one will enjoy the company and hospitality of one's favourite double act, Mr Whyte and Mr MacKay thank you very much"!

Off Hughie went to join the queue at the bar armed with our first supply of drink tickets.

Suddenly a voice rang out, it was Tommy,

"Are you entering any of the competitions Harry"?

"I might as well". I replied. "Put me down for the Dominoes and Pool".

"What about the synchronised swimming event"? He said jokingly.

"Oh, I'll give it a miss for tonight Tommy, my bikini top has a rip in it anyway"! I replied back.

During the events of that evening, I was beaten at the Dominoes, that bloody double six beat me every time.
Anyway, I was waiting to take part in the Pool games.

Whilst sitting there, draining every drop of the amber liquid from my refillable glass, with my brother Hughie seated alongside me, a greasy long haired male, wearing a bright blue coloured jacket with the sleeves rolled up to the elbow, in order to reveal several pieces of what appeared like 'barbed' wire, wrapped ever so ridiculously around his forearm and to crown it off was the large brass crucifix dangling around his neck, it was that heavy, I would reckon within six months he would resemble the 'Hunchback of Notre Dame' with a Dowagers' Hump.

He sat down in the chair beside me and said,

"So are you on the buses too"?

"No"! I replied.

"Oh right". He said, as he nodded his head. "What do you work at then"?

"I'm a lorry driver". I responded.

His eyes opened wider, "A lorry driver"? "I've always wanted to be a lorry driver. What kind of lorries do you drive then"? He enquired.

"A Scania 110". I answered.

"A Scania 110"? "That's my favourite lorry of all time. How long is it and how many wheels does it have"?

Now, at this point I'm thinking, this guy is just out for the day, where's his psychiatric nurse.
He was obviously a lump of wood in an earlier life!

Anyway, I turned to Hughie and on seeing my facial expression, Hughie got up from his seat and walked over to another bus driver friend and said,

"Here Archie, yer mental brother is annoying oor Harry, so ye better have a word with him and tell him to do a 'drum' roll and 'beat it'.

As Hughie returned to his seat on the opposite side of me, Archie signalled to his brother to come over and said,

"See that bloke yer talking tae, he's a Polis, so don't annoy him, awright"?

Conversation finished, Archie's brother comes back over and sits down on his seat next to me. He then composed himself, looked both ways and behind himself, before staring me right in the face. He then winked and whispered in a low voice out of the side of his mouth.

"I always wanted to be a Polis"!

At which point, I turn my head around to look at Hughie and Hughie said under his breath,

"Lean your head forward as if to pick up your pint and I'll just 'hook' him".

As it turned out, he was quite a nice lad, although slightly demented. Also, apart from the 'barbed wire' wrapped around his arms, posing as some sort of modern jewellery, he had a set of motor vehicle 'battery' jump leads tied in a neat knot around his neck like a fashion statement.

"Why the jump leads around your neck"? I asked him.

"I forgot that you needed to wear a tie tonight and these were all I could find in the boot of the car"! He replied.

"Aw well"! I said. "You better not 'start' anything in here"!

Hughie then spotted the buffet being uncovered on the display tables by Big Andy Hunter, nick named 'Billy Bunter', he was enormous and rumour had it that he was originally a triplet, but he ate the other two.

When he was at school, his favourite instrument was the 'dinner bell'.

Hughie moved swiftly to the front of the queue and shouted over to me,

"Harry"! "Do you want 'Toad in the hole' wi' some salad"?

"If you don't mind Hughie, I'll just have the salad, I've been 'towed in the arse' once and didn't really enjoy it"! I responded.

The assembled queue of drunken bus drivers laughed in unison.

Much later, after the buffet was cleared away and many, many more whisky's were consumed by yours truly, I was summoned to the pool table to play my first game.

"Right Harry", said the organiser. "Your on this side with the rest of the 'OMOs' here".

"Ho"! I said, taking great exception to this remark, then Hughie explains that he means 'OMO' (ONE MAN OPERATED) bus drivers and not 'HOMO' as in a sexual preference.

Surprisingly, with Hughie's coaching skills, I win it very easily. My next couple of games go the same way, as I find it all so easy.

The balls as they say, are running kindly for me and are never to far from a 'pocket' to pot into.

I'm playing like Stephen Hendry, minus his 'plooks' and before I know it, hey, I'm in the semi – final stage of the tournament and I find it very hard to believe, because, I can hardly see the pool table, never mind the coloured balls.

Anyway, my opponent 'breaks off' and I'm bent down, lining up my cue for my first pot at a ball.

"Hold it Harry"! Hughie said, "Pot this one first"!
I looked over to see one of my balls covering a pocket and just perfect for potting.

"I never noticed that one, thanks Hughie". I replied back.

The game continued in this vein for several shots, me bending down to line up a pot and Hughie changing my mind by pointing out a much more easier pot to take on. 'I must have drunk more than him'!

All the time Hughie was talking one load of utter 'pish' to my opponent, who was having to use all his concentration skills, just to understand what Hughie was saying to him.

As for me, I'm closing one eye and trying to focus on my cue ball as it appears to be moving about the table on it's own and I'm thinking to myself, 'I wish that bloody white cue ball would stop moving'!

Then just as I am about to take my shot, I clearly see a hand lift up one of my balls and place it in front of the pocket.
I straightened up and composed myself, because I decided, I must be seeing things, balls don't move about by themselves and even in my rapidly drunken state, I couldn't 'piss this mot'.
I mean I couldn't miss this pot!

Then I realise why I'm so good at pool all of a sudden.

My brother Hughie was talking to my opponents and while distracting them he was placing my balls over the pockets for me to pot them, as well as 'potting' a few of my balls into his own trouser pockets.

I wondered how some games seemed to be over very quickly .....
I was only potting half my quota of balls, compared to my opponents' full quota.

Being a conscientious Police Officer with a reputation for being fair and upholding the law, I couldn't handle the fact that I was in the Pool Final, due to the behaviour of my brother Hughie who was blatantly cheating. With this playing on my mind, I did the only honourable thing available to me!

No I didn't own up, are ye daft? I was winning. I just compromised.

I told Hughie I didn't want his help in the final because I was good enough to win it on my own.

Suffice to say, I didn't win the final and to rub salt into my wound, I played total crap and was completely 'whitewashed'.

Come to think of it, even when I play sober, I'm total crap.
Which, in retrospect was probably a fair result for me.
However, Hughie reckoned I was lucky to get nil!
Which was hurtful, because I do have feelings you know!

In the meantime, during the evening, Hughie had also been helping the Committee, by handing out the drink raffle tickets as well as helping himself to several sheets for doing it.
He had also arranged with the girl behind the bar, to allow us to trade them in for a 'carryout' and had placed an order for a Bottle of Whisky, Bottle of Rum and two dozen cans of Red Stripe lager.
Just in case we got thirsty on our road home.

I decided we should go for a 'Chic Murray', an Indian curry and told Hughie I was going outside for some fresh air, while they were clearing up.
Unfortunately, I forgot to mention to him about going for the 'Chic Murray'.

While sitting on a wall outside waiting for Hughie, a Police 'Panda' car pulled up alongside me.

"Hi Harry"! Said the passenger, "What are you doing here"?

"Oh hi Davie"! I replied.

It was a friend I had been to College with. I continued. "I've got this theory Davie that the world revolves on an axis, so if I wait here long enough, my house will pass by and I'll get hooked up by the wife"!

"Don't think so Harry, why don't you jump in the back and we'll give you a lift"? He said.

"Okay Davie". I said, getting into the rear of the car.

"Could you drop me off at the 'Noor Mahal' Indian Restaurant in Shawlands, I feel like a wee 'Chic Murray' afore I go home"!

"No problem Harry"! Replied Davie and he promptly drove me to the Restaurant dropping me off outside the front entrance.

As I entered I was shown to a table for two as I had told them that my brother Hughie would be joining me here.
All I remember after that, was the waiter nudging me and saying,

"Excuse me Harry, but we are wanting to go home now and I don't think your brother is coming"!

I looked around me and the restaurant was empty, apart from the staff, who were still clearing up.

"What time is it Zaffar"? I asked the manager.

"Very late Harry, quarter to one in the morning, you have been sleeping for ages"! He replied.

While all this was going on, Hughie had come out of the club looking for me, couldn't find me and organised a small search party of his friends to help him search the nearby golf course, just in case I had fallen into a 'bunker'.

Having no success in finding me, he then flagged down a 'fast black' taxi and went to my house, where he informed my wife the following,

"I've lost him, I've lost Harry. One minute he was there and the next minute, 'Poof' he was gone".

Mind you, 'Poof' I think was the wrong choice of word to describe my disappearance from outside the club.

He continued explaining,

"I've been up and down the golf course next to the club looking for him in case he fell into a hole"!

"Some of the guys helping to look for him nearly shit themselves and ran off when they saw me dressed in white coming towards them in the darkness"!

All the while, my missus stood with her arms folded, listening to this pathetic tale of woe from my drunken brother and totally unconcerned.

Poor Hughie, he was completely demented and unaware, that I was wrapped up, as snug as a bug in a rug, in the spare room of my parents house and snoring away like the proverbial pig, with my runners up medal for the pool competition along with a 'crisp' twenty pound note tucked away in my breast pocket.

Roll on the next games night on the buses!

'Fares Please'!

'Canteen Patter'

Big Eddie, a police motorcyclist called at the Force Training Centre canteen.
As he approached the 'Hot Plate' counter, he asked the female assistant Cathy,

"Have you got a plate of yesterdays soup"?

To which Cathy replied,

"Certainly Eddie! Come back tomorrow"!

'German Knockers'

Several years ago, my partner and I were engaged in Motorcycle Patrol Duties, when we were instructed by the Duty Officer of the Division, in which we were working, to check all the local schools in our area, due to an ongoing complaint of vandalism.

With this in mind, we went out on our Police patrol.

A short time later, whilst travelling along a road in Glasgow, I observed two males and a female, loitering outside the gates of a school there.

We about turned and headed back down towards the school, whereby, one of the males, who was wearing a black 'cowboy' hat, had climbed over the metal railings into the school and along with the other male, was attempting to assist the young female, who was wearing a black 'mini' skirt and a 'bikini' style tee shirt, barely covering her rather large 'bust' and revealing a very 'bronze' tanned midriff.

As we pulled up alongside them, I enquired what they were doing in the school grounds.

One of the males answered me in a 'broken' English accent,

"Vee are German Students and vee stay in zee school, yah"!

"Oh, so you're Germans"? I replied.

Then as I looked over at the well-endowed, buxom breasted young female, I thought I would be smart and said,

"Your wee 'bird' has got some pair of knockers for her size"!

To my complete and utter embarrassment, the young female replied in a broad Glaswegian accent.

"Hoh You"! "He's bloody German, no' me"!!

Exit very quickly two red faced Police Officers!

'Is That Right'?

An ex-cops son applied for a position in the police as a civilian Force Station Assistant, working in the front office, dealing with members of the public.

After receiving several 'knock backs' for the post, his father decided to write to the Police Personnel Department for an explanation as to why he was not being considered.

He received a written response a few days later from the head of the Personnel Department stating that his application had contained too many 'speeling' mistakes.

'Another Vacancy'

An advertisement for a Police cell van driver, added the special qualities they required,

'Working alongside Police Officers, you are expected to be of a high physical fitness and prepared to deal with occasional bouts of bad temper and anti social behaviour'!

They forgot to clarify from whom did this paragraph refer to?

'The Smell of Robbery'

In the early eighties, due to an increase in 'Armed' Robbery in the Strathclyde area in particular, the Police decided to set up 'Special Anti Crime Teams' in order to try and combat them.

I was enrolled as a member of this section and our objective was, whenever the Police radio operator broadcasted a certain 'Codeword' over the 'air', followed by the location.

Along with my colleagues involved in this section, I would respond immediately at 'High Speed', to the location of the call.

However, this entailed a lot of patience, watching and waiting.
In order to pass the time, I began to make up my own 'Code Names' for the various teams of Police Officers involved and came up with the following abbreviations;

F.A.R.T. ; Which will stand for, **Fast Action Response Team.**

S.H.I.T. ; Which would stand for the C.I.D. or the **Strathclyde High Intelligence Team.**
Hence the expression, the C.I.D. what a load of shit!

Then I came up with,

C.R.A.P. ; Which would refer to the **Criminal Response Action Patrol.**

You should by now, see the direction in which I was heading and especially where my thoughts were coming from.

Another which readily springs to mind is,

A.R.S.E.S. ; They were the **Anti Robbery Squad Enquiries Section.**

Finally, the last section I came up with was,

P.O.O.F.S. ; Who have absolutely nothing to do with the team you're maybe thinking about, or who readily come to mind, they are the **Police Operational Order Form Section**, who will deal with all new legislation resulting from the enquiries performed by the other Crime Teams. (They're the 'back up' team!)

So please, don't even whisper under your breath what you think of it, for I'm just as likely to make up another squad from your expression and it's even more likely to be accepted!

Mind you, what I should have said was I've just got 'wind' that they're still recognised as 'Farts' within the Police having recently been informed that the '**FART**' Team was still the term being used.

'<u>Speeding Excuses</u>'

The 'speed' radar unit stopped a car for exceeding the limit.
As they spoke with the male driver and made him aware of the offence, his passenger wife insisted in interrupting the police officers at every opportunity about how surprised she was that her husband should be stopped for speeding rather than her.

"I can't believe he has been caught breaking the speed limit, because he is a Funeral Director and is used to driving slowly. Now if it had been me driving, I could understand because I'm always speeding about in the car"!

The reporting officer then interrupted her and said,

"Well if you'd like to wait until I'm finished with your husband, I'll be delighted to take down your full confession in writing"!

'Help the Aged'

One day whilst engaged on uniform beat duty, I saw an elderly woman, struggling with several heavy grocery bags.
Being a considerate police officer, I went over to her and said,

"Give me your bags hen and I'll carry them for you".

"Oh thanks son, that's kind of you, I'm just up here". She said, pointing to an old tenement building.

I carried them all the way and it was just my luck, it was a 'Tap Dancer'. Up I went, all the way to the top floor and when I got to her door, she thanked me very much and said,

"That was awfy good o' you son, would you like an orange"?

"No thank you missus"! I politely replied.

"Well"! She said, "Would you like a wee hauf"?

I thought for a second, then answered,

"I would love a hauf"!

To which she responded,

"Right then, you hold it while I go and get a knife"!

'Graffiti'

I attended to a call from an 'Asian' grocer's shop, regarding a complaint of 'Graffiti', sprayed on his security shutters.
On arrival, I met with an excited 'Mr Singh', the shop owner, who spoke with me at 60 MPH. (That's very fast!)

"Woh! Slow down Mr Singh"! I said, "Take a breath man"!

"I am being very sorry Mr Harry, but I'm also being very angry with these bastards who do this" He replied.

You could say he was not a happy 'chapatti'!

He then led me back outside his shop and pulled down his security shutters, to reveal in 'bold' writing, a 'metre' in height, the letters **'NF'**!

"Look sir, look what they have done"! He pleaded.

I looked at it for a moment, then said,

"C'mon Mr Singh, you're not seriously suggesting that 'Nick Faldo' was here last night, spray painting graffiti on your security shutters, because, I know for a fact he has an alibi, he was playing golf in America, 'cause I saw him 'live' on the TV last night"?

He looked at me with a puzzled expression and said,

"No, not Nick Faldo sir, but, 'National Front' bastards!

I looked straight at him and replied with a wry smile,

"Nick Faldo"? "National Front"?
"I personally suspect it was 'Nick Faldo', 'cause the 'National Front' aren't clever enough to spell 'En Eff', but what do you think yourself Mr Singh"?

He stood staring at me for a moment, then a smile broke out across his face and he laughed,

"Okay dokey Mr Harry, I'll wash it all off"!

As I left him, I said,

"You do that Mr Singh and I'll keep my eye on that bugger 'Nick Faldo' just in case he comes back tonight, okay"!

'Don't Call Me a Liar'

One time in the witness box of the Sheriff Court, I was being cross-examined by a very young inexperienced Defence agent. During his questioning of me, he said,

"I put it to you officer that did not happen and what really happened was ,.,.,. He then began to give the court a very different version of events.

He then looked at me for a response, so I said, "Are you calling me a liar"?

Quick as a flash, the presiding Sheriff 'jumped' in,

"Eh! I don't think Mr Ross is saying that, are you Mr Ross, you're not calling the Police Officer a liar"?

To which Mr Ross, the defence lawyer, surprised and somewhat flustered by my response to his scenario, said,

"Certainly not M'Lord, I was only giving an alternative version to the Police officer, but I have no more questions for the witness"!

'Paton's Place'

While a guest at 'Stuart Paton's family party, I noticed a relative of his going to the kitchen several times and returning each time with a glass of 'lager' and a whisky.

I also observed that he did not appear the worse for the amount he was drinking.

The next time he returned from the kitchen with a replenished 'glass' in hand, I remarked for all to hear,

"Hey 'Big' man, you certainly like your bevy, I think you must have hollow legs, if I drank as much as you, I'd be legless"!

There was silence for a moment, then the assembled party of guests burst into hysterical laughter.

What was funny about that then, I thought to myself?

Then Stuart informed me that his relative had an artificial leg!

Talk about putting your foot in it!

However, as if that wasn't bad enough, I later told a joke about leaving for school one morning and when I returned home, my family had moved house.
Again there was silence, followed by hysterical laughter.

It transpired that one of the females at the party had suffered the very same scenario, which I had related in my joke, and to crown it all off, she just happened to be married to the guy with the artificial leg.

There's nothing like keeping it in the family!

'TV Detectives'

On particular nightshift, about half past one in the morning, I was walking 'the beat', along the Cathcart Road, in Glasgow, with my partner 'Joe Doris', when we were stopped by a 'taxi driver', who informed us, he had picked up a male, carrying a large 26 inch television set, in the Langside area and dropped him off at a tenement close building in Govanhill, Glasgow.

We both agreed this was suspicious circumstance indeed.

The taxi driver took us down to the area where he had dropped him off and pointed to the tenement building that the male had entered carrying the television. He also provided us with a full description of our suspect.

We entered the tenement close and one by one, we listened outside the door of each tenant.
We performed this procedure at three doors, when 'bingo'! At the fourth door, we could distinctly hear a male and female talking. More so the female, who was saying,

"Don't leave the auld wan there, I'll fall o'er it during the night when I get up for a pee"!

'Could this be a television she was referring too'?
Well we thought so.

They sounded like they were in the hallway, close to the front outside door.
I knocked on the door and immediately heard the male say to her,

"Don't answer it, let's just keep quiet"!

I knocked on the door again and said,

"Can you open the door please, it's the Police, we know you're in there, we can hear you talking"!

Next thing I heard was something being dragged towards the rear of the outside door.

"Open the door or I'll force it"! I said.

By this time, 'Joe' had gone to the back of the tenement building and climbed up to the rear window, where he saw the male dragging a set of bedroom drawers into the hallway, obviously to 'barricade' the front door and prevent us from gaining entry.

I informed him, we knew what he was doing and advised him to open the door voluntarily, or we would have to forcibly open it.

"Just hawd yer hoarses"! The female shouted, I then heard her saying to the man,

"Open the bloody door, I don't want it 'kicked' in wi' them bastards, they sound a bit 'gung ho' tae me"!

Moments later, the door was opened and inside, in full view, was the 'suspect' stolen television with pride of place on the 'sideboard' within the living room area.
Several questions later, the male suspect was still vehemently denying having stolen it.

Then, the wife said, in typical 'Glesca' fashion,

"Aw fur fuxsakes Boaby, tell 'em where ye 'blagged' it afore they empty the bloody hoose intae the street and dae us for no' havin' a TV licence as well"!

He then relented and told us, he had stolen it from the bar lounge of a well-known Southside hotel.

Apparently he waited outside the open window for over an hour until the residents, who were all drinking, eventually retired to their rooms for the night. Then he climbed inside the open window and promptly removed the television.

As a footnote, the residents who were drinking and whom he referred to, turned out to be nine C.I.D. Detective Police Officers, who were staying at the Hotel, while attending a 'Detective' Officers course at the Police Training School in Glasgow!

Oops! Not exactly the best of starts to their 'Detection' course.

'The Glasgow Sheriff Court'

There was a particularly well-known Sheriff in Glasgow, who was renowned for his 'hard line', on what may be described as the 'Neds'!

On this particular day, he entered his Court, which was crowded with Lawyers and the general public.

As he surveyed his court, his attention was drawn to a scruffy young male at the rear of his Court, who did not stand to attention like everyone else when he entered.

Instead, the insolent young 'ned', continued to lounge in his seat, with his hands thrust in his pockets, chewing loudly on a piece of gum!

The angry Sheriff summoned his Court Usher and said,

"Kindly inform that young man at the rear that I will not tolerate 'mastication' in my Court"!

The bemused and more than confused Usher walked back up the Court to the youth and said firmly,

"Right you – the Sheriff says you've tae get yer hauns oot yer poackets, ya dirty wee bugger"!

'The Sheehy Report'

Several years ago, the Police Force was to undergo radical changes, as far as the serving members were concerned, with the arrival of Sir Patrick Sheehy and his proposed 'Sheehy Report', for the Police.

The Police Federation, who represent the Force Members, held what was commonly referred to as a 'Greeting Meeting', in order to discus some of the aspects of the forthcoming report.

During the meeting, various questions were asked and unsatisfactory answers given.

At this point, one of the Police Officers near the front of the hall, who was totally disillusioned by all that had gone before, stood up and said,

"Correct me if I'm wrong, but I believe the 'Sheehy Report' implements many changes to the Police Force as we know it"?

"That is correct". Replied the Federation Representative.

"Well"! Continued the Officer. "I'm convinced that all these sweeping changes have taken place and you as our Federation, representing the rank and file, have not opposed a single point. In fact, I would go as far to say, all you have done, is dilute them"!

He then paused for a moment, then said, "Allow me to provide you with an example of how I see it"!

"It appears to me, that if the 'Sheehy Report' had said, 'All serving members of the Police Force will stand with their heads in a bucket of 'shite', for ten minutes every shift'.

You, the Federation, would have considered it a victory, if you had it reduced to five minutes per shift"!!

'Ill Health Retiral'

I was summoned to the Divisional Commanders office.

"You want to see me sir". I asked.

"Yes Morris", he said, "I'd like you to retire for health reasons"!

"But I'm not ill, sir"! I pleaded my case.

"Maybe not", he said, "but you make me sick"!

'That's Entertainment'

A few years ago while performing with a Scottish Folk Band, we were playing a concert at a local theatre.

During the performance a fight broke out at the rear of the hall and a bottle was thrown from the back, which struck a man on the head, sitting in the front row.

Concerned for the man and the injury to his head, I jumped off stage to give him first aid.

"Are you alright mate, are you alright"? I enquired.

Without looking, the man quickly replied,

"Naw I'm not! Hit me again, I can still hear them"!

'The Tasmanian Devil'

During the World Pipe Band Championships being held at Bellahouston Park, in Glasgow.
I was engaged in Motorcycle Patrol duties within the park, when a young man, dressed in full Highland Regalia, Tartan Kilt and all, approached my partner John Knox and myself and explained that he was a serving Police Officer from Tasmania, visiting Scotland, to take in the World Pipe Band Championships.

He then asked if he could take a photograph of John and I, on our Police Motorcycles, to which we readily agreed.

He then began to set up his camera, using a light meter and changing the lens and filter.

While doing all this, I interrupted him and suggested he take his photograph from the opposite side, whereby, he would also include all the competing pipe bands in the background and their variety of coloured tartans on display.

"Good idea"! He said.

He then proceeded to check the lighting again changing the camera lens and filters for the new angle I had suggested.
Satisfied he had the correct lighting filters fitted, he began to focus the camera on us.

He then knelt down on the grass to capture his prized photograph, when 'Bonk'!
In true commando style kilt wearing, I witnessed a most unexpected surprise, as down from below his kilt and onto the grass, dropped his rather well endowed 'penis'!
This was definitely a 100% genuine Tasmanian Devil!
If I didn't know better, I'd have sworn it was eating the grass!
As it was, it certainly appeared to be eating something!

At this point, two elderly women were passing and one of them was taking an interest in what was happening with us.

On seeing the aforementioned exposed Tasmanian Devil in full view and in full colour, she grabbed hold of her friends arm and in the loudest 'whisper' I've ever heard, she said,

"Peggy! Peggy! Quick! Would you look at the size o' that big beauty, is that no' a belter of a monster"!

Peggy turned around and looked on in amazement, then said to the young photographer,

"I bet you're not from around here son"?

"No Mam". He replied in a proud voice. "I'm from Tasmania"!

"Of course you are and you're obviously eating the right things 'cause you're a fine specimen of a boy"! Peggy said.

"Why thank you Mam"! He said happily blushing.

"Bye the way"! Peggy said. "You almost gave Cathy a stroke"!

"No he didnay"! Interrupted Cathy, then in a wicked 'girlie' voice she said, "but I wish he would have"!

Both women then walked off giggling like a pair of naughty young school girls.

As for our Tasmanian Police Colleague, he was none the wiser as to what he had done or the unexpected thrill he had bestowed upon two elderly Glasgow 'spinsters' on a day out, strolling in the park!
I often wonder, thinking back to that day, if that is why all photographers use the saying,

"Watch the Birdie"!

'Legless in Auchterarder'

Whilst attending the Police Convalescent Home in Auchterarder, Scotland, I met up with a remarkable Police Officer from the Royal Ulster Constabulary in Northern Ireland, called 'Billy'!

Billy had tragically lost his right arm, from above the elbow and his left leg, from above his knee, in an IRA 'Bomb' explosion, while on his Police Patrol.

Despite the 'loss' of his limbs and the obvious pain and discomfort of wearing Artificial Limbs, Billy showed a wonderful outlook in life and had an amazing sense of humour.

One night, during our time together at the home, Billy and I had gone out for a few drinks. However, a few became several, as we relaxed in the local Hotel Lounge, exchanging funny jokes and stories.

Before we knew it, the Bar Lounge was closing.
I decided to have, 'One More Drink for the Road', while Billy went to the toilet.

As I sat there waiting for Billy to return, I realised, he was taking quite a while and his physical condition, coupled with the amount of drink we had consumed, he may have fallen over.
I went to the toilet to check on him, but to my surprise, there was no sign of Billy.

As I walked outside the Hotel, I saw Billy, lying 'flat' out on the roadway, trying unsuccessfully to get up.

I ran over to him and said in a concerned voice,

"Billy, are you okay"?
Billy replied in his broad Irish Brogue,

"Of course I'm not okay Harry, I'm fucken legless"!

As both of us began to laugh, I looked over and saw Billy's artificial leg, lying on the other side of the road.

Apparently, Billy tried to kick an empty 'Coke Can' lying on the footpath and his leg 'shot' off across the roadway"!

'Football Crazy'

On another occasion, John Reilly was involved in Policing the 'Old Firm' Derby Football Match, within Celtic Park in Glasgow. This involved him walking around the perimeter track during the game and preventing any 'Hooligans' from running onto the field of play, or throwing any objects.
As John walked around, he couldn't avoid watching the game and being a keen Celtic Supporter, he was becoming more and more anxious, as time ticked away and his team 'chased' an equalising goal.

Three minutes to go until full time and Celtic 'bundled' a goal in from a goalmouth scramble.
As the supporters went wild with excitement, John got caught up in the hype of it all and threw his Police hat into the air!

With his arms raised in ecstatic celebration, the swirling wind within the enclosed stadium, caught his hat and carried it onto the centre of the field of play, whereby, one of the Rangers players, retrieved it for him.

The Police Football Commander, having witnessed John's reaction to this made sure John never, ever worked at another football game in which Celtic were involved.

'Face Like A Fish Supper, All Chips'

I had just left Pitt Street Police Headquarters on my Police Motorcycle and was riding it along the Clydeside Expressway.
I had overtaken several vehicles on my way back to the Police Traffic Garage Depot.

As I approached another vehicle in front of me, I noticed it was wavering slightly from side to side and the driver appeared to be acting very suspicious.
His head was 'bobbing' up and down and he looked as though he was doing something, other than concentrating on his driving!

I decided to pull along side the drivers window and have a look for myself.
Just as I was almost at the rear door of the car, the driver's window opened and a 'newspaper', full of potato 'Chips' was discarded out the window, all over me and my motorcycle!

That was it! I activated my Police 'Siren' and 'Blue Lights' and signalled the 'startled' driver, to pull over and Stop!!
I'm positive I saw him mouth off in his interior mirror, "Ohhh Shittt"!

I got off my motorcycle and dusted myself down, of the loose 'chips' and walked towards the car.

The driver gave the impression, he would have liked the ground to open up there and then and swallow him and his 'Chips'!

However, having a sense of humour, I had to see the funny side. So rather than 'charge' him with an Offence, I stopped all the Traffic on the Expressway and made him walk back along the carriageway and pick up every 'chip' he hit me with, when he discarded them out the window!

Fortunately for him, I had already eaten the 'chip' that was on my shoulder!

'Pieces of Pizza'

From "The Adventures of PC Archie Bauld"

PC Archie Bauld walked into a 'Fast Food' shop and ordered up a 'pizza'.

"It'll be about fifteen minutes"! Said the assistant.

"That's okay"! Replied Archie.

He then waited, while it was cooked.

When it was ready, the female assistant asked Archie,

"Would like it cut into four pieces or eight pieces"?

Archie replied in all seriousness,

"You better cut it into four hen, I couldn't eat eight pieces"!!

'Tulliallan Barbers'

New recruits at Tulliallan Police College have found a way to grow their hair longer, without the Instructors noticing.

Apparently they're getting their ears pulled out further!

'BRiNG BACK HANGiNG AND HAVE A SWiNGiNG TiME'

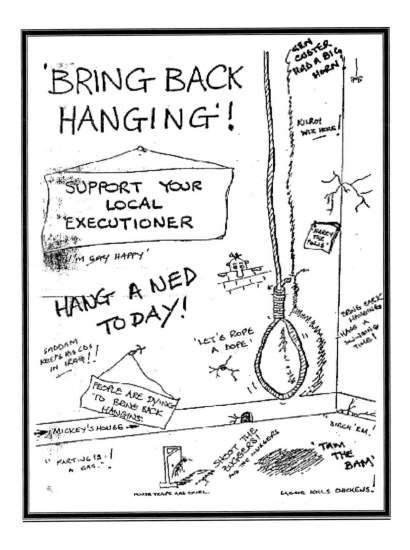

'HARRY THE POLiS'

'<u>You Said It</u>'!

Along with my partner, we called at a Southside Motor Repair Garage, to organise a repair to his car.

The garage 'Boy', (I use that word loosely) who swept up the floors and ran some errands for the owner, was an old likeable 'Dosser' called 'Jack Barnes', who had a drink problem, but unlike many of his drinking 'buddies', his brain was as sharp as a tack.

"If yer looking for the Boss, he's no' in yet"! Jack said in his usual 'gruff' voice.

"That's okay Jack, we'll just wait"! I replied.

After a few minutes, we decided to have something to eat, so I said,

"Jack"! "Could you nip around to the 'Greasy Spoon' Café and get me, two rolls with scrambled egg and two cups of coffee"?

"Aye, nae bother"! Said an obliging Jack.

I then handed over a £10.00 note and said,

"Get something for yourself Jack"!

A short time later, Jack arrived back and handed me the coffee and rolls, then pushed the 'change' into my hand.

As I put the coffee and rolls down, I checked my change.

"Ho Jack, £2.60 change, where's the rest of my money"?

To which Jack replied in his gruff voice,

"Ye told me tae get something for mysel', so I bought a half bottle o' wine"!

My partner and I just burst out laughing.

Old Jack Barnes didn't have a 'Scrambled' brain, that's for sure!

'Housebreaking'

A cop is late for work one morning and arrived at the office, just as the shift is being detailed their duties by the Duty Sergeant.

"Sorry I'm late Sarge, but I came home last night to find my apartment had been 'tanned'!!

The entire shift is stunned by this news.

"How did it happen"? Asked the concerned Shift Sergeant.

To which the cop replied,

"The wife left her 'sunbed' on all night"!

'Reducing Crime'

The Chief Constable of Strathclyde, working in conjunction with the various Regional Councils, has devised a plan to help reduce the amount of crime on our streets by 50%.

Apparently they're going to double the number of streets!!

'No Chance'

Constable Paul was absolutely delighted when he won the tickets for the Hospitality Suite at Ibrox Stadium to watch his favourites Glasgow Rangers play a league game.

His prize also included a four-course meal, Champagne and other refreshments at half time and full time.

In order to enjoy his day out, he wakened his wife, who was in bed after a busy nightshift duty and asked her to drive him to the stadium to drop him off.

Barely awake and wearing her pyjamas, his wife duly obliged.

Afterwards, as she drove back home, she realised, she had no keys to get into the house and made her way back to the stadium, where she had to make her way through the football supporters, to the Stewards at the front door of the main entrance.

"Excuse me, but I've just dropped my husband off for the game and I haven't any house keys, could you possibly give him a call over your loudspeaker 'tannoy' system, to come to the front door with his house keys"? She asked.

"Certainly love. What's his name"?

She paused for a moment before uttering the words,

"It's John Paul"! She then said. "But I can assure you he's a Rangers Supporter"!

The steward looked at her and said,

"Hen! This is Ibrox Park, Glasgow. If I broadcast the name 'John Paul' over the 'Tannoy' system, he'd get lynched afore he even reached the stairs"!

"Well what do you suggest I do then? I'm locked out"! She asked.

"Go home and call the Police". He suggested.

"I am the Police and so is John Paul"! She responded. "Anyway! They'll just 'boot' the door in. I know what their like". She added.

"Well why don't you go home and 'boot' the door in yersel' and claim some overtime"? He replied condescendingly.

As it was, she made her way home and spent the remainder of the day, in her pyjamas with her neighbour, until finally a drunk, but extremely happy 'John Paul' returned from his hospitality day out, totally unaware.

'Don't Trust the Polis'

A number of crimes have taken place recently, whereby the suspect involved, was a 'bogus' Police Officer.

An alarmed Senior Officer was prompted to issue a statement to the public, informing them, not to trust anyone claiming to be a Policeman!!!

'How Did They Know?'

This was in a newspaper years ago,

'A man discovered in a car with his trousers down at his ankles and a woman astride him, was arrested today for impersonating a Police Officer'!!

'Jacket in'!

It was the practice while working within the 'Production' Department of the Police, to note the Time, Date, Locus, Crime / Offence and full description, of all items worn or involved in incidents and 'Lodged' as Productions for the Court.

At the completion of the Court Case, where they were produced as part of the evidence, the Procurator Fiscal's Office would issue a 'Release Notice', in respect of the items retained by the Police.

It was then the duty and responsibility of the Production Officer, to notify the owner of the item, for them to call at the Police Office and collect them, within a certain time.

This would result in a 'Recorded Delivery' Official letter, being sent to the named person's address, claiming to be owner.

After a certain length of time and all attempts to have the Owner, call and collect having failed, then the articles, such as clothing, referred to on the notice are destroyed.

On one particular occasion, I was clearing a serious 'back log' of clothing items, where I had a 'bag' for destroying and a 'bag', for a local Church Charity Group, who were collecting warm clothing and blankets for 'Bosnia' Aid.

Any warm or half decent items of clothing, I came across for disposal / destruction, I would put into the 'Bosnia' Aid Charity bag!

Several weeks later, having dropped off the 'Black Plastic Bin Bags' of clothing items at the church, I received a telephone call from a young man, requesting the return of his confiscated jacket. I checked the relevant Property Book regarding his request, but could find no information as to the whereabouts of this particularly distinctive jacket, in his name.

He explained, there were complications in his request, in as much as he was not the person wearing it at the time, when the Police had retained it as a Production.

He then stated, the jacket was being worn by his cousin, at the time of the offence and therefore, it would be lodged by the Police, under his relative's personal particulars.

I then looked under the name and address of his cousin and sure enough, I found it, but unfortunately for him and to his utter disappointment, it had not been reclaimed during the 'Retaining' period, after the owner had been notified by the 'Recorded Delivery' system and therefore, as per force instructions regarding unclaimed items, it had been destroyed.

The caller 'blew his top' big time!

"Destroyed"?

He shouted down the telephone.

"Destroyed my arse, you're winding me up big man"?

"I can assure you sir, I am not"! I replied. "The named owner, who according to the records was your cousin, was contacted by Royal Mail, 'Recorded Delivery' several months ago, to contact this Office and arrange for the collection of the jacket. He failed to do so within the retention time"!

"But it's my jacket"! He said.

I responded, "And"? But before I could finish, he interrupted.

"It's a big bloody bright Orange 'North Face' jacket, worth over three hundred quid (£300.00) you couldn't miss it"! He said aggressively.

"Well, I'm sorry, but I would take it up with your cousin and ask him why he didn't call to collect it when he was notified by recorded delivery"! I replied.

He then responded.

"Are you for real mate"? He enquired. "You're telling me, you've destroyed a three hundred quid 'North Face' jacket"?

"Not at all sir, I'm telling you, I destroyed an big Orange coloured jacket belonging to your named cousin. How much it cost, I don't know. How fashionable it was, I couldn't care less. So, I suggest you speak with him about it"!

I then replaced the telephone.
However, this entire episode of events prompted an interested response in me.
Thereafter, every night, when I watched the Television News or a Humane Relief Documentary, where 'Aid' workers were involved, I was always conscious of the fact, that some poor wee 'Refugee' guy, was walking about, with a three hundred quid, bright orange 'North Face' waterproof jacket on, none the wiser of it's make, expensive value, or even the fact that it's all the rage in the 'yuppie' fashion scene, but just extremely grateful and delighted to be keeping 'warm' and 'dry' in the freezing cold!

'Cruelty to Girlfriends'

Sitting in the Police canteen, I was joined by the office cleaner.
As she sat down beside me, I was reading an article from the newspaper,

"How disgusting can you get? I remarked. A man's been charged with indecent behaviour towards a nanny goat, is that no' terrible"?

To which the cleaner replied, "Not really, it sounds a bit like my son and his new girlfriend"!

'The Carbolic Alcoholic'

As a raw recruit in 1972, I was 'farmed' out to work the Oatlands area, near to the Gorbals.
I was partnered off with an old cop, with several weeks of his Police service remaining, before he officially retired.
As I was leaving the 'Muster Room', after being detailed my duty, another young cop approached me and enquired.

"Are you working with 'Soapy', Harry"?

"Soapy"? I said, shaking my head. "No, it's Davie I'm working with"!

"Soapy"! He said. "That's his nickname".

"How come"? I enquired.

"You'll see"! He then laughed and walked off.

Davie had been a real character and a Police Officer with a great track record, however, due to the recent death of his wife, Davie had struggled to overcome her loss and found solace in alcohol.

On this particular Sunday afternoon, Davie took me out with him to meet the gatehouse man at a local factory, in our area.
I thought we were there for a cup of tea, but Davie and the gatehouse man had other ideas and were pouring and drinking something that was the same colour, but entirely different.

A short time later, we received a call on our personal radios, that the shift Sergeant and Inspector, were requesting our locus position, to rendezvous with us.

Davie answered the radio and began making 'screeching' and 'burping' noises, which didn't make any sense, but sounded like distortion.
He then turned to me, grabbed his hat and coat, then said,

"Quick Harry, follow me and run like hell"!

We ran halfway down the road, when the radio controller broadcasted,

"Would the station trying to transmit please note you have a poor signal with a lot of interference, suggest you change your position and try again"!

Further down the road, Davie stopped and transmitted his 'screeching' and 'burping' noises again over his personal radio.
He then looked over at me and catching his breath, he heaved a huge sigh, then said,

"Right, go"!

We were off again down the road until we came to the bottom of Polmadie Road and Old Rutherglen Road, where there was an old fashioned 'Police Box'.
(Remember them, 'Doctor Who' and all that?)

Davie put his key in the lock and opened the door for us both to enter, he then stood for a moment inside, while he tried to catch his breath, then he put his hand behind the 'Box' telephone and produced a polythene bag, with what appeared to contain pieces of 'Tablet'.

I watched him as he then took a piece of the tablet out of the bag and 'popped' it into his mouth. He began to chew vigorously.

The smell emanating from his mouth was revolting and as if that wasn't enough, a yellow foam coloured 'bile', began to pour profusely out of either side of his mouth, as he continued to chew on the tablet.

"What the hell are you eating Davie"? I enquired, while screwing my face up in utter disgust at the stench.

"It's Carbolic soap son, guaranteed to mask the smell of the best 12 years old Scotch whisky"! He said confidently, while still spouting foam from his mouth like a 'rabid' dog and dripping uncontrollably down his uniform tunic and onto the floor.

"Carbolic soap"? I said. "Are you serious"? "You're breath is absolutely bowfin man and you look as if you've got Rabies"!

"Maybe so"! He said. "But you can get disciplined for smelling of drink, where as, you can't get done for smelling of soap"!
With that statement, he tapped the side of his nose with his forefinger and winked an eye.

"Do you think so"? I replied. "Well you should get done for just being minging"!

Just at that point, we could see the Supervisors approaching us.

Davie, put his bag of 'soap' tablets back behind the telephone box, emptied his mouth of foaming spittle and wiped his lips with the sleeve of his tunic, before leaving the Police Box to greet them.

It took me all my time not to laugh, as Davie conversed with the 'Gaffers' unaware, he was still 'slobbering' at the mouth.

As for the 'Gaffers', they were just desperate to get away.

I learned a big lesson that day, never drink on duty and you won't have to wash your mouth out with 'Carbolic' like 'Soapy' and also to pay particular attention to the nicknames of your partners, the clues are there!

Such as, 'Gattling Gub', (Talks non-stop) 'Olympic Flame', (Never goes out) 'Sergeant Signal' (The Tube with the Stripes), 'The Itch' (Gets right under your Skin) and 'Harpic' (He was clean round the bend)!

The following day, I was partnered off with 'Big' Dick Bruce!!

'I'm Sick! Sick! Sick! Up to Here'

I followed a car that was being driven in excess of the 30 m.p.h. speed limit, down a particularly busy and accident 'black spot' roadway.

Having covered the required measured distance, I activated the police car 'blue' lights and 'siren', to signal the female driver, to pull over and stop.

Once stopped, I walked up to the driver's door.

The female driver was sitting inside, staring directly ahead.

I asked her to open the window, but she ignored my request.
I then opened her door myself and as I did, the female driver, then 'vomited' all over her steering wheel and dashboard.

She was so worked up and nervous at being stopped by the police, she made herself so physically sick, she couldn't stop 'spewing' all over her car.
Therefore, I reckoned if I didn't make a hasty retreat, she would be spewing all over me as well.

Having witnessed her obvious distress, I decided under the circumstances that a 'warning' would suffice and allowed her to carry on her way!

Bye the way, she was also totally 'minging' wi' the vomit!

'Michael Schumacher – Not'

One early morning, while attending a call along with other Police mobile officers, in the Old King George 5th Dock, in Govan.

My partner Graeme Povey was putting up a case for our Ford Consul GT, being faster than George Dalglish and David Ball's, new Jaguar 4.2.
George 'baited' Povey that he would leave him trailing in his wake, if they both had to race to an emergency, since he had a 'Jag'.
The inevitable was decided that we would have a race along the old 'derelict' dock roads to see which car was the fastest.
We lined up alongside each other, then, 'go', we were off, hurtling along the 'cobbled' dock roads at great speed.

Graeme managed to edge our car in front as we approached the winning post.

I looked back with great relief and delight that my underwear was still unsoiled and was about to wave 'bye, bye' to George and David, only to see them 'juddering' to a sudden stop, as smoke appeared from the engine of the 'Jag'.

What could have happened, I hear you ask?

Did they 'blow up' the engine? ….. No!

The Jaguar has considerably less ground clearance than most cars and as a result, while hurtling along, George had straddled a metal stud, which just happened to be the remains of a 'Capstan', (Not the cigarette)!
Whereby, the engine 'cross member' of the Jaguar was caught by the protruding 'stud' and virtually removed the whole engine, as the momentum of the Jaguar bodywork went forward, causing considerable extensive damage to the 'Jag'.

This was an incident that required some expert 'storytelling' from the car crew!

'Vasectomy'

Several years ago, having made the decision, not to have anymore children, I reluctantly agreed to go for a 'vasectomy' operation. Although, slightly apprehensive about it.

The doctor tried to allay my fears by saying,

"A wee snip here and a wee snip there and Bob's your Auntie! So to speak"!

However, my sinister in law, (That's what I call her) added her 'tuppence' worth to my concern. Just to make me feel better. "It's a dawdle for a man. You don't feel a thing"! She stated.

I responded by saying,

"Is that right? And you would know from experience I expect, having been a man in an earlier life"!

'You'll have guessed, I don't get on with her! (Him)!!

----------------/////----------------

'Moustache You a Question'

While serving my Police probation period at the 'Gorbals' Police Station, City of Glasgow, I turned up for the first night of my five weeks nightshift 'duty roster', sporting a rather feint but visible 'Pancho Villa' moustache.

The guys had informed me on my shift that if you want to grow a moustache, you either do it on your annual leave or during the nightshift.

This was the present trend of style of facial hair and I must admit, I thought I looked darn well 'cool for cats' so to speak!
I sat in the 'muster room' along with the rest of my police colleagues, awaiting my duty detail, 'stroking my face' like a veteran 'moustache grower' and making sure I drew attention to it, just in case someone present hadn't noticed.

There were the usual remarks, "Something up with your lip Harry"? "Could you no' wash yer face afore you came out to yer work son"?

At the end of the 'rib taking' and 'muster', I was summoned to Inspector Wilson's office.

I knocked on his room door and was instructed to enter.
As I did, I was asked the following,

"What is that on your face Harry"?

"It's a moustache I'm growing sir"! I replied, rather pleased with myself.

"A moustache"? He said. "Well, take that Harry"!

He then handed me a 'blue' form.

In all my innocence, I thought, I had to fill it out in order to state my intention and obtain permission to grow my moustache.

"What's it for sir, permission to grow it"? I asked in all innocence.

"No"! He replied. "It's a resignation form, if you think you suit the moustache, fill it in"!

'Baldy old Bastard'!

'Toilet Graffiti'

I had to laugh one evening when I entered the toilet, used by 'suspects' brought to the office for interview.

One had written,

"My mother made me a poof"!

Underneath it, someone else had written,

"If I send her the wool, would she make me one"?

'Road Accident Excuses'

'I had been shopping for plants all day and was on my way home. As I approached the intersection, a large hedgerow sprang up, obscuring my vision and I collided with another car, which I did not see'!

'Taxi to Charing Cross'

While performing surveillance duties in the Serious Crime Squad, I was following a certain car being driven by the 'target' male, along a busy roadway in the City Centre of Glasgow.

At this time, I was driving a black 'hackney' taxi, which we used, from time to time and I was the 'tail end' in the surveillance team, operating that day.

I was then contacted by radio, to 'close up' on the 'target' and take over the main role, while the 'lead' vehicle was replaced, to avoid any suspicion by the suspect 'target'.

As I moved up through the traffic on the 'target' vehicle, I was stopped in a line of vehicles at an automatic traffic light junction.

While waiting for the 'lights' to change and move on, I was watching the target vehicle closely, for any sudden manoeuvre movements from him, when suddenly, the door of my 'taxi' opened and a well dressed 'suited' male got into the back seat.

"Charing Cross please driver"! He said.

I turned around to look at him and said,

"Sorry mate, I'm not for hire"!

"Well your lights on, so you'll have to take me"! He replied.

I looked over to see the opposite junction traffic lights change to 'red' and turned back to my 'passenger'.

"Right mate, you'll have to get out"! I said. "I'm busy"!

"I beg your pardon"? He enquired.

"You heard me, get out the taxi"! I repeated.

"You're for 'hire' and I'm hiring you to drive me to Charing Cross"! He said rather indignantly.

"And I'm telling you to sling yer hook and get out my taxi"! I replied in a stern voice. "Now move yer arse and hurry up about it"!

"That's it! You've gone too far, now I'm going to report you"!

He responded in true 'Basil Fawlty' fashion. Then, taking a 'notebook' and 'pen' from his breast pocket, he began 'scribbling' notes down.

By this time, the traffic was starting to move off and I'm being instructed over my police radio,

"Right Harry, move up, move up, the target is now yours"!

Now I'm getting really annoyed, so I said to my passenger,

"Right mate, write this down, 'I am personally going to 'batter' you, if you don't get out my taxi right now'. Comprendi"?

"That's it, so you're threatening me now with violence, you are in such deep trouble my man"? "They'll throw the book at you"! He replied, while writing in his notebook.

"Harry, will you move up on the target before the traffic lights change again"!

Came the next instruction, 'blasting' loudly over my police radio.

This was the final straw, my patience was exhausted and I opened my drivers door.

"That's it, you've had your chance"! I said.

I jumped out of the driving seat, opened the passenger door and grabbing hold of his 'jacket collar' I physically pulled him out of his seat.
At this point, he wrapped his arms around the passenger 'handlebar' rail and held on tightly, refusing to 'budge'.

"I'll call the police"! He said, clinging on like a leech.

"Don't bother, I'm here"! I said. "Now do yerself a 'Rodney' and piss off"!

I then threw his briefcase and 'brolly' onto the footpath before he would move.

I got back into the taxi and drove off into lead position, where I continued with my surveillance of the target vehicle.

However, as I looked back, I saw my passenger 'flag' down another taxi and get in.

I had to laugh, when I thought of the 'taxi' driver asking,

"Where to mate"?

And him replying,

"Follow that cab"!!

'The Snitch'

It is common knowledge amongst the rank and file that a well known Senior Police Officer got a young Policewoman into trouble.

Apparently he reported to a Traffic Warden, she was parked on a double yellow line!

'A Special Unit 'Burns' Supper'

Several years ago, while working in 'Crime Intelligence' at the Police Headquarters, Pitt Street, Glasgow, I attended a 'Burns Supper' evening of entertainment, held in the HQ restaurant.

There were some excellent speakers at this well attended venue and the top table was littered with senior Police Officers and distinguished guests, due to the fact, the main guest speaker was none other than a high profile and colourful character, who was a former 'Conservative MP' and highly respected Queens Counsel.

It was delayed in starting, due to the late arrival of our distinguished guest speaker, who was absolutely 'pished' as a 'fart' and 'decked' out in his usual tartan three-piece suit.

As the senior officers and other invited guests squirmed in their seats at his 'noisy' and over the top entrance, some of the top table had to lend assistance to him, as he swayed unsteadily, on his feet.

After a brief 'slurred' apology, which I struggled to make 'head nor tail' of, it was his big moment, to address the 'Haggis'!

The 'Chef', carrying the 'Haggis' was led in by a tartan clad 'bagpiper' and made his way along the front of the top table, stopping directly opposite 'the speaker' and placing the impressive 'haggis' in front of him.

'Drams' of Malt whisky were then handed around the top table of guests, before 'the main speaker' began his most infamous and totally unforgettable 'address to the haggis'!

He began with thus,
"As a former well-known 'Special Unit' client of mine in Barlinnie once said", (pausing for a moment to compose himself), he then blurted out loudly,

"Take that, you bastard"!

He then began stabbing and thrashing the large knife into the cooked haggis before him.

Pieces of Haggis was being strewn everywhere, all over the table.

The expressions on the faces of Senior Officers at the top table were speechless.

As for the assembly seated before them, of which I was one, we howled with laughter, at his antics.
However, a few minutes later, it was a case of, 'Taxi for Pitt Street', as he was whisked off into the night!

'Pea And Ham From A Chicken'

My sister Linda invited me over for a Bar-B-Q one summers day and I volunteered to do the cooking.
I was making chicken drumsticks, sausages, burgers and pork chops.
After I had finished cooking, Gary, my sister's young son, helped himself to a large pork chop and went out to the front of his house, where he joined my daughter and his friends.

"Whit's that you're eating Gary"? Asked one of his pals.

"It's a pork chop"! He replied 'smugly'!

"Where did you get it from"? Asked another friend.

Gary replied sarcastically, "From a 'cow', stupid"!

At which point, my youngest daughter 'Kimmy' said,

"No Gary, from a 'pig'…. Stupid"!

'C.S.I. Glasgow'

How does 'Gil Grissom' and his C.S.I. team do it, week after week, they solve the crime on TV.
It's one thing solving it and another thing convincing a jury, particularly a Glasgow jury, to convict the accused, on the D.N.A. evidence available.

One particular case in the High Court in Glasgow comes to mind, where an accused male, serving a 'jail term' for 'robbery', attended the High Court for trial, on another charge of 'armed' robbery.

During the trial, we heard that the accused, along with another male, both wearing ex-President 'Richard Nixon' masks, had entered a bank, produced a 'gun' and 'robbed' it.
While 'holding' up the bank, an ex police officer, standing in the queue, decided to have a go at the gunman and began to struggle with him, during which he pulled off the gunman's mask, exposing his true identity.

Meanwhile, the other robber with the money ran out of the bank and drove off in the 'getaway' car, leaving the gunman stranded.
The gunman, then ran along the busy Main street, pursued by the ex policeman, who shouted at a male 'shopper', to 'stop him'!

The shopper put down the message bags he was carrying, but on seeing the 'gun' in his hand, he stepped out of the gunman's way, allowing him to pass unchallenged.

The gunman managed to escape capture at this point, but was later identified and arrested, along with the gun used, which was recovered in a shoe box within his house.

Now, the 'farce' of a court case went as follows;

The ex-cop, who 'had-a-go' with the now accused gunman in the bank and 'ripped' off his 'Richard Nixon' mask, positively identified the accused male in the 'dock' as being the same person he had fought with.

The male 'shopper', who was carrying his bags of messages, when he heard a call to 'stop' him and was about to intercept, when he noticed the 'gun' in the hand of the accused and side stepped him.
However, he positively identified the accused in the 'dock' as being the same person and said,

"When someone is running towards you and passes within one metre of you armed with a handgun, you don't forget what the person looks like"!

Next up, was the cops who 'raided' his house and arrested him, they found the handgun, used in the robbery, concealed within a 'shoebox' and during his taped interview with the C.I.D. he freely admitted having bought the 'Richard Nixon' masks used, while on a weekend trip to Manchester.

Then, the final 'nail in his coffin' was the 'Scene of Crime' evidence.

Enter the 'Forensic' Scientist, to give his expert evidence.
Yes, just like C.S.I.'s Gil Grissom on Channel 5 TV!

He was the C.S.I. officer who matched the D.N.A. on the hair follicles, which were ripped out of his head, when the accused struggled with the ex-cop in the bank and lost his mask during it.
The forensic officer then gave the 'odds' of one in five million, that it wasn't the accused person on trial involved.
In other words, it was the accused male seated within the dock!

The jury went out to deliberate and consider the evidence, before returning a short time later with a **'Not Proven'** verdict!

As for the accused, he couldn't stop laughing at the jury decision.

"THE ADVENTURES OF PC ARCHiE BAULD"

BY 'SEAMOR TOONS'

'A Side Order Of Vegetables'

A very funny guy was a Detective Superintendent called Charlie Craig.

I had been fortunate to hear Charlie as a guest speaker at a function and found him a very 'witty' character.

One time, whilst a guest speaker at a 'Burns Supper', held at Police Headquarters in Pitt Street, Glasgow, which was attended by the Deputy and Assistant Chief Constables, Charlie was speaking about the honour of a Knighthood, bestowed upon the present Chief Constable, at the time.

Charlie went on to say that the Chief Constable had invited his most senior staff members, who just happened to be seated along either side of Charlie at the top table, to accompany him for meal and a celebration drink.

Once inside the restaurant, the Chief Constable and his party, were escorted to their specially prepared table.

After they were all seated, the waitress noted the 'drinks' order, whilst a second waitress handed out the food menus.

After a few minutes the food menu waitress returned to note each individual guest's food order.

She began with the Chief Constable,

"Now sir, what would you like to eat"? She asked politely.

"I'll have the 'fillet mignon', please"! Replied the Chief Constable.

The waitress made note of his order, then asked,

"And what about your vegetables"?
To which the Chief Constable replied,

"Oh, they'll just order for themselves"!

Only 'Cheeky' Charlie would attempt to get away with that one!

'Exam Results'

During the Police Scotland Examinations, a police officer was taken aside by the Adjudication Officer and informed, he was being reported to the Examination Board for cheating.

"Who me"? Said the surprised officer. "Where did I cheat then"?

The Examiner replied, "Question eight"!

"What about question eight"? Asked the officer.

Well said the Adjudicator,

"The person sitting on your immediate right has written his answer as, "I don't know"!

And you've written, "I don't know either"!!!

'Kicking the Habit'

A male was arrested and on being searched, was found to be concealing 'drugs' within his training shoes.
When asked to explain his possession of the drugs, he gave the following excuse to the officers,

"I'm genuinely trying to kick the habit"!

'Red Card For Pink Slip'

A regular complaint within the Police was the amount of time, members of the public, would call at the office, to report having lost a bag, wallet, handbag or it's contents.

At this point, I would stress, on most occasions, it was usually, the loss of a 'cashed' Dept of Social Security 'giro cheque'!

With this in mind, they would ask for a 'pink' slip / loss report, to present it to their insurance company, in order to make a claim, but more realistically, if you were on 'State Benefit', you could take it to the D.S.S. office and obtain help with your loss, i.e., a 'crisis loan', etc.

This procedure was regarded as being 'abused' big time, by certain members of the public and was highlighted with a story in the 'Sunday Mail' newspaper, under the heading, **'Red Card for Pink Slips'** and referred to the amount of 'false reporting'!

Whilst on duty one Sunday evening, a woman called at the office to report having lost her handbag and could I provide her with a 'loss' report for her insurance company.

Having heard it all before, I handed her a copy of the 'newspaper' and advised her to sit down, read the article and consider the consequences before I processed her request.

I sat back down at my desk and continued with my paperwork.

After a short while, I looked up to see the woman, still 'peering' at the 'newspaper'. Thinking she might be illiterate, I said,

"Do you have a problem reading the article missus"?

To which she replied, "Not normally sir, but my reading 'glasses' were in my bag when I lost it"!

'Ask Him Yourself'

Out together one day on motorcycle duty with 'John Imrie', we were patrolling the Great Western Road area of Glasgow, when John and I had occasion to stop a van, being driven by a young Asian male, regarding an expired 'tax' disc being displayed.
As the van pulled up outside a 'mini market' grocer shop, the young driver, got out and went to enter, but was stopped by John.

The driver stated the van belonged to the shop owner and he was just the delivery driver, he also gave his name as Iqbal Singh.
While John spoke with the driver, I went inside to speak with the shop owner and check the identity of the driver of his van.

I immediately noticed the shop owner was wearing a 'ring' with the name 'Iqbal' on it.

"Can you tell me your name please"? I asked him.

"Iqbal Singh"! He replied. "I am de shops owner here"!

"Can you tell me your drivers name"? I enquired.

"Ass' him, sir"! He replied.

"No, I don't want to ask him, I'm asking you"! "Now what is his name"? I said with a stern voice. Knowing the driver had given a false name to John.

Again, the shopkeeper replied, "Ass' him sir"!

Losing my patience, I replied,

"I told you I'm asking you not him"! "Now tell me his name"?

This time with his voice trembling, he replied,
"Ass' him sir, Ass' him"!

"That's it, this is your final chance to tell me his name, or else"? I said with authority,

"I'll charge you with attempting to pervert the course of justice".

To which the 'poor' frustrated shopkeeper answered,

"Ass him sir"! "Assim Naseem"! "Honest"!

'<u>Talking Sex</u>'

A black policeman I worked with, was employed with the 'Support Unit', which consisted of a van occupied with usually eight or ten officers, who would be deployed into a troublesome area.
One evening in particular, a certain officer nicknamed 'Gattling Gub', was berating him in the van in front of the other officers and making him the 'butt' of most of his jokes and remarks.

Later that evening, half of them were dropped off at my office for their refreshment period.
As they all sat around the table, enjoying a cigarette and a cup of coffee, one of the officers said to the black officer.

"Why did you put up with that 'tosser' Gattling Gub slagging you off, why did you not just tell him to shut the fuck up"?

The black officer, totally calm and sitting quietly, looking down at his coffee and replied,

"Because, at the end of the day, I know something he doesn't"!

He then paused for a moment before continuing.

"When his wife worked as a cop with me, I had oral sex with her before him"!

You could hear a pin drop at this remark, then as one, the entire table of seated cops burst into hysterical laughter!

'Who's Comforting Who?'

'George' had arrived at my office from the 'Drug Squad', where he had worked for several years and as you can imagine, had seen some 'memorable sights' during his time working there.
We both had the same years in service and on one particular day, we were detailed to work together.

During the shift, we received a 'death' message to deliver. This was the sudden death of an older man, who had collapsed in the street, whilst attending the local Post Office.
His elderly wife, who had remained within the family home, had to be informed.

As usual, in these difficult circumstances, you call at a relative, a neighbour or a friends house, to accompany you to the family home and assist in comforting the person, whom you are about to inform with the sad news, of the death of a 'loved one'.

Unable to trace a relative, we called at her neighbour's house and explained the situation.
The neighbour, who was also a close friend of the elderly couple, was devastated at the news, but, was prepared to accompany us, to inform the wife of his death.

We knocked on the door and the wife answered it.

"Hello Mrs Brown, I wonder if we could come in a minute, we have some sad news to tell you"? I said to her.

"If it's about 'Paw Broon', he's at the shops getting a few messages, but he'll be back shortly"! She said in all innocence.

"Well, it is about 'paw' hen, but I'm afraid it's not very good news"!

By this time we had walked through to the living room area. With the assistance of her neighbour to comfort her and put an arm around her, I broke the news of her husband's sudden death.

There is no easy way to perform this task! No book has ever been written, describing how to go about it and it doesn't matter who you are, a family members death is devastating!

The poor woman was distraught, the tears and 'cries' of disbelief, greeted us, as the neighbour, with visible tears in her eyes, tried, along with George to console her.
I decided to make a 'cup of tea' for her, while the others were comforting her.

As I was doing this, I noticed there was no milk. I told the neighbour, who said for me to go into her house and get some from the fridge in the kitchen.

What a 'shock' there was for me when I returned to the 'grieving' woman's house.

There in the middle of the 'sofa couch', was my police partner George, 'sobbing uncontrollably' and being comforted by both the bereaved woman and the neighbour.

Looking at the situation involving all three of them, you'd have thought George was the one who had just received the 'bad' news.
The older woman had her arm around George, 'petting' him 'sympathetically' and saying,

"It's okay son, just let it all out and don't be embarrassed"!

I couldn't believe what I was seeing! I was lost for words!

So I blurted out the first thing that came into my head.

"That will be three cups of tea then"?   "Milk and sugar everybody"?
Later, once George had drank his tea and composed himself, he told me that in his 23 years police service, this was the first time he had ever delivered a 'death message', to a 'loved one' and the built up emotion of it all, just 'hit' him!

"Promise me, you won't say anything to anyone about what occurred today"! He pleaded with me.

"My lips are sealed George"! I replied, as I drew my fingers across my lips, as if to close a 'zip' fastener.

However, the nickname, '<u>Greeting Face</u>', stuck with him for the rest of his Police service!

Till this day, George thinks I said something; but I can assure him I didn't!

'I wrote it down'!!

'**Road Accident Excuses**'

'I had been shopping for plants all day and was on my way home. As I approached the intersection, a large hedgerow sprang up, obscuring my vision and I collided with another car, which I did not see'!

'**Police Proverb**'

My kids handed me a 'Key Ring' one Christmas, which said,

"Help your local Policeman, 'Beat' Yourself Up"!!

'Forgot Who You Were Today?'

Whilst patrolling with my partner 'David Ball', we stopped a vehicle, being driven along Edmiston Drive, opposite 'Ibrox Park' in Glasgow.

The driver, who was Asian, accompanied us around his car, while we examined it for any obvious, visible defects.

We asked him to identify himself and to provide some form of proof.

The driver immediately pulled out his wallet, containing some personal papers and handed me a driver licence, bearing the name 'Abdul Singh', and stated he was the named 'licence' holder.

While examining it, David noticed that the drivers licence had not been signed by the 'holder' and pointing out to him that it was an offence, he handed it back to the driver, along with a pen, to 'sign' it.

The driver took possession of his licence and proceeded to sign it, 'Mohammed Al', then suddenly, realising the error of his ways, he 'scored' it out with the pen and began to write above it, 'Abdul Singh'!

His lapse in concentration in forgetting who he was that day, cost him dearly, but I 'bet' he won't forget who he is next time he gets stopped by the Police!

'The Bar-L Strike'

During the strike by prison officers at H.M.P. Barlinnie in Glasgow, they were refusing to take in anymore prisoners during the dispute.
As a result, the prisoners were being 'housed' at Police Offices, such as London Road.

Many Police Officers from the various Divisions around Glasgow were detailed to report there for their duties. The duties being, we were to perform the job of the Prison Warden.

Let me inform you immediately, both jobs are completely opposite and entail a different approach.
We had to allow them certain privileges, not allowed in the 'Bar-L', in order to prevent any unwanted 'disturbances' or 'rioting'!

However, whilst involved doing this, I spoke with some of the prisoners and have enclosed a few of the conversations.

Alec ; "I'm 58 years of age and I'm a 'lifer' in installments".

"I've served 26 years in prison for 'drink' related offences like 'Breach of the Peace', 'Drunk and Incapable' and 'Shoplifting', all stupid things because of my alcohol problem".
"I'm safe in here, because I can't handle the outside, I'm frightened"!
Alec died shortly after his release, his death was 'Alcohol' related.

Ian ; "It's my first time in prison and I got locked up for 'Litter'! I threw a lousy 'chip' poke away".....

'You don't get locked up for 'Litter', I said.
"You do if you fail to pay the fine"! He replied.

Tam ; "My 'Brief' said, it's only 'Breach of the Peace', just plead 'Guilty', everybody's getting a letter to return to Court after the Prison dispute is resolved.

You won't be sentenced today!

So what happened? With his expert advice, I pled 'Guilty' and was sentenced to 30 days"!

Later the same evening, Tam shouted out, "Hey Boss, any chance of a wee stretch"?

I shouted back, "You've already got 30 days Tam, is that not enough for you"?

'Is that a Cannon I Hear?'

A young struggling actor was contacted by his agent and offered a part, in the London West End stage play, 'Waterloo'!
The part was small, but the pay was very good and would guarantee him some much-needed work, for several months.

On accepting the offer, he was sent his lines to learn and told to come immediately to London. With his bags packed, he was off.
As he travelled down on the train, he tried out various voices to deliver his lines, "Hark! Is that a cannon I hear"? "Hark! Is that a cannon I hear"? "Hark! Is that a cannon I hear"? "Hark! ......
This dress rehearsal of his lines continued all the way to the stage door of the theatre, arriving minutes prior to the start of the play and his stage entrance.
He was quickly whisked off to make-up and wardrobe, dressed in costume and ready to walk on stage, with minutes to spare.
As he received his cue to make his entrance on stage, he took several steps, when suddenly there was an almighty **'BANG'**!!

Receiving such a fright! He totally forgot his opening lines and blurted out loudly,
"WHAT THE FUCK WAS THAT"?

'Trailer Bike'

One day while out on motorcycle patrol, I passed a 'cash and carry' for gardening needs and advertising a 'closing down' sale!

During my lunch break, I went in and it was 'Christmas' for me. Everything you'll ever want at ridiculously reduced prices, I just had to have some of this.

"I'll take six bags of that and four bags of this and four of your 'Rowan' trees, oh! And give me four of your wild birdhouses and three packets of birdseed. Is that grass seed and lawn feed? I'll take some of them and two tins of fencing preservative paint and a hard garden brush"!

They even had that new 'Whyte and MacKay' grass seed. You scatter it over your lawn and it comes up 'Half Cut'!!
Anyway, after they had totalled up the cost and I paid for it, I asked,

" What time do you close and I'll come back and collect my goods later"?

"Sorry mate"! He replied. "We're closing now, you'll have to take it all with you"!

"Arrghh! Shock horror"!

Out I went to my police motorcycle and loaded the six bags of compost across the back pannier boxes, grass seed and lawn food in the pannier, bird food and boxes in the other pannier, paint tins, balanced on top of both panniers, held by the weight of the compost bags, potting compost across the petrol tank and I carried the trees and brush in one hand!

Down the road I went with my bike camouflaged like a landscaped garden with my bargains.
Just as I was turning into the motorcycle shed, I was passed by my Superintendent in his car, who almost crashed, as he spun his neck around like 'Linda Blair' from the 'Exorcist' for a look!

Later, I was reprimanded and the next day I received a 'memo note' from him, instructing me to attend the motorcycle garage to have a trailer fitted to my bike.

'Remind me of Reminsky'

On hearing the news that a film is to be made about the life of the famous 'safe' breaker, 'Johnny Reminsky, I was reminded of a short story I was told by a Detective Inspector.

As a young police probationer, he was patrolling his 'beat' one night and checking out property in the area.
Whilst engaged in this duty, he went around the rear of a Post Office in Paisley Road, Glasgow, when he heard something.
He quickly shone his torch up in the direction of the noise and saw a man sliding down a drain-pipe at the rear of the building.

As he drew his police baton, the man said, "Calm down son. You've caught me fair and square. I won't give you any trouble"!

On reaching the ground level, he immediately held his hands out in front to be handcuffed by the young cop.
What a surprise to learn later, he had apprehended the 'famous' gentleman safebreaker and war hero, 'Johnny Reminsky'!

Apparently Johnny was serving a prison sentence during the war and was released by the Authorities to help the war effort.
He was flown to Germany, behind enemy lines with specific orders to break into certain 'safes' and steal enemy secrets!

By all accounts Johnny performed his duty to his usual perfection and proved, 'No Safe was Safe' from 'Johnny Reminsky'!!

'Marmalade or Jam'

I was fortunate to visit Moscow in Russia several times and struck up a relationship with a local 'Moscovite' called Vitaly Mironov, who was a Historian and the President of the 'Moscow Caledonian Society'.

One evening, whilst participating in a little 'drinky poo' of the local 'vodka', Vitaly told me a story about one of the first times he visited the United States of America.
He had frequented a bar diner near to the hotel where he was staying and became the centre of attention with the regulars present.

The conversation got around to sex and one of the American 'hippy' style guys, who had joined the company, asked Vitaly, what methods they used when making love in Russia?

Vitaly, trying to sound interesting and knowledgeable to his new American 'friends', said in his best Russian 'broken' English.

"I always use preservatives, I enjoy sex better"!

"Preservatives"? Asked the 'hippy' guy, surprised by this.

"Yes", "Preservatives and in Russia, we have many types and fancy flavours"! He said, rather pleased with himself.

Several more drinks later, he made his excuses and headed back to his hotel for the night.

The following evening, he went back to the local bar diner for a drink and as he walked in the 'joint smoking hippy' guy, who had been part of his company the previous evening, shouted out,

"Hey 'Boris', I tried your 'Russian' way of having sex last night, it was amazing man, my woman went wild"!
"She loved the 'strawberry' jelly the best"!

However, now, with a better knowledge and command of the English language, he informed me he meant 'preventative' sex, as in a 'condom', as opposed to 'preservative', as in jam!

'Karaoke? Not'

A certain Police Officer, aptly nicknamed, the 'Slug', because he was so slow at everything he attempted, was attending the Sheriff Court in Glasgow, in order to give evidence at a trial.

While in the witness box, he was being cross-examined by the accused Defence Agent.

The officer answered each question that was asked of him, in his own immutable fashion, refusing to allow himself to be harassed or hurried.
This was becoming infuriating to the Defence Agent, to such an extent, he said abruptly,

"Do you know Constable, you give the impression of being more laid back than 'Perry Como', would you agree with that statement"?

To which the 'Slug', reacted by shrugging his head from side to side and giving the question some consideration, before replying,

"I'd probably have to agree with you sir, so long as you don't ask me to sing like him"!

'Road Accident Excuses'

'I pulled away from the side of the road, glanced over at my mother-in-law and headed over the embankment'.

'<u>Mini A Bargain</u>'

Being recognised as a bit of a 'scatter cash', there was no expense spared when I purchased my first motorcar.
There it was, in the paper, circled with a fancy '3D' dimensional box with a bold highlight heading, stating, 'Bargain Of The Week'!

I liked the name right away, a 'Morris' Mini, brown in colour and all for the princely sum of, £30.00. ..... 'Cash', from the 'Executive Cars Centre', Paisley!

The pungent smell of 'dampness' should have been an obvious clue, but I accepted the salesman's patter,

"Can ye no' smell that leather upholstery"? "Man, ye just canny beat the Real McCoy"? He enthused.

"And another extra feature fitted, is the sporty 'bucket' seats"! He added.

They were certainly 'bucket' seats alright!
Saturated with water and the metal rimmed handle still attached!
There was a 'Hole In Dem Buckets, Dear Henry, Dear Henry'!

The radio wasn't working, but he put it down to a faulty 'valve' or maybe a 'short' wire!
In other words, I think there was a 'wire – less'!

"Don't worry sir, we'll replace it"! He said with an air of confidence.

"Are we paying by cash or would you like credit arrangements? He then enquired.

"None of your 'HP' credit payments for me", I said. As I handed over hard cash! £6.00 of which was made up with crisp new 10/- shilling notes from my pay packet.

With the ignition key in my hand, I jumped into the drivers seat and started it up!
In an instant, I noticed there was no 'Va'! Va'! 'Voom'!
It was more like a 'buzz', 'buzz', 'buzzz'! for a brief moment I thought there was a 'wasp' stuck up the exhaust pipe, but no, that was the noise from my 'souped up' (clapped out) engine.

"Just listen to that engine man, it's purring like a cat'!

Said the 'drooling' salesman with his 'syrup of fig' hairpiece, slightly askew.

'Purring like a cat' my arse, it was more like 'squealing like a pork belly pig'!
The noise emanating from under the 'bonnet', suggested a slack fan belt! Or in my case, probably a slack 'snake' belt!

Even the valid M.O.T. certificate was a duplicate. The examiner obviously didn't believe it the first time!

However, I put all that to one side as I drove out onto the main road.

Let's see what she can do, I thought. Nothing to sixty, (0 – 60 mph) in eight the salesman said, he forgot to mention 'days' and not seconds.

I should have remembered and old saying of my fathers, 'the only good thing about Paisley son, is the main road leading out to Glasgow'!
Well I was on it and I was eager to 'burn' some 'rubber'.

Forget 'Michael Schumacher'! He was just a 'Cobbler' from the Govan area when I was at school.

With the 'pedal to the metal', I was off in a large 'puff' of smoke, so much so, I actually expected a 'Genie' to appear and grant me three wishes.
Like, I wish I had an engine, I wish I was a mechanic and thirdly, I wish I had a brain!

Well it was the 'Pantomime' season after all. (Oh yes it was!)

Having been on the road now for just over thirty minutes, enough time to go there and back on a bus and driving 'full out', I saw a sign for Glasgow.
The art of prayer really works.

Now, I know a 'Mini' engine is not the most powerful, but this one of mine, couldn't pull a sailor off yer granny! Suffice to say, I would have been hard pushed to pull the skin off my 'Ambrosia' creamed rice!

A man and woman on bicycles and an old woman, pulling herself along in a 'wheelchair', overtook me twice!
With one leg and a punctured tyre!

Come to think of it, maybe the holes in the floor of my car were for your 'Doc Marten' feet to go through, so you could run and make it go faster! Then again, maybe they were for the 'braking' system.

Suddenly, it began to rain quite heavily and I switched on the windscreen wipers ... nothing! Zilch! Zero!
They didn't work and as the rain got heavier, it became more difficult to see the road ahead.
Drastic times require drastic measures, as I rolled down my drivers window, put my hand out and grabbing hold of the wipers, began operating them manually, thrashing them up and down the windscreen.

'Not recommended'!

To cut a very long story short, I decided not to hold onto it for too long.

'Depreciation in value and all that'.

So, while I was a student at the Police College, Tulliallan, I was offered the chance to purchase another 'Mini', this time from a Sergeant 'Colin Robertson', who was a College Instructor.

This one was in good 'nick', or as they say in Glasgow, it was 'minted'! So, after checking the window wipers worked properly, I bought it!

Here I was, twenty-one years of age and the first two-car family in the street. Mind you, there were only two houses, it was an awfy wee street I lived in.
Was I becoming an obsessed collector of cars, I thought?

As it was, 'Dougie Mack', a fellow student was also looking for some form of transport and practically 'begged' me to sell my 'manual' operated Mini.
Without twisting my arm up my back, I managed to convince him, to talk me into selling my 'passion wagon'.

"Okay"! "Okay"! I said, reluctantly, "Give me thirty quid cash and she's yours"!

"Why call it she"? "Cause it was an absolute 'cow' in the morning"! Plus the rest of the entire day I might add.
I had to 'tinker' about with the engine every time I tried to start it.
It was like performing 'foreplay', before I could get it to do anything!

However, Dougie was a single guy and had money burning a hole in his pocket.

I couldn't help but smile, when driving down the motorway on my way home from 'Tulliallan' Police College, for the weekend, when I was overtaken by Dougie, waving away frantically and 'blasting' the horn with excitement, as he passed.
I think that was the first time it had passed anything.
I tell a lie, it passed water the day the radiator hose burst, but there lies another story!
However, returning to the Police College on the Monday, I had to laugh, when I asked Dougie how the car was running and he informed me, it had been 'scrapped'!

"Scrapped"? I said, somewhat hesitant and surprised.

"Aye, I gave a 'burd' a lift home from the dancing on Friday night and as I was reversing backwards, I bumped into an 'Audi Quatro' in the car park and bashed in the drivers door.
That cost me an arm and a leg. He said.

"What about your damage"? I asked.

"My damage"? He replied. "The bloody 'sub-frame' collapsed, but the 'burd' was a darling, so, I ignored it and drove along a country road and 'parked up', in a field for a wee 'winching' session, while we listened to 'Wet', 'Wet', 'Wet'".
"As it turned out, it was more like 'Pish', 'Pish', 'Pish'!
"The rain became heavier and poured down".

"Later, as I went to drive away, the ground was that soft with all the rain, the bloody 'Mini' had sunk and was up to the 'axles' in mud".
"Stuck fast in the mud, I had to call out a recovery vehicle company, who proceeded to 'rip' me off along with the rest of the sub-frame, as he 'towed' it out of the field".

"Total cost for my weekend, thirty quid to you for the motor, a hundred quid to the Audi driver for the damage to his door and forty quid for the recovery driver and as if that wasn't enough, I never even got my Nat King Cole"!!

As he stood staring at me, I said sympathetically,

"Ah well Dougie, some people are just lucky with cars"!
"Some people are just lucky in love"!
"But unfortunately for you Dougie"…..,

I paused for a moment, then said,

"You've just got too much money"!

'Don't Talk To Strangers'

One day I was sitting within the front lounge of my house, having a glass of wine with my new next-door neighbour.

Suddenly, the front door to my house opened and in walked my youngest daughter, carrying an armchair.

A few minutes later, she was followed by my other two kids, who were carrying a three seater sofa between them.

I enquired where the items had come from?

To which my eldest daughter replied,

"A man gave them to us"!

I immediately got up from my seat and proceeded to 'scold' all three of my kids.

"What are you doing"? Asked my shocked and surprised new neighbour.

To which I replied.

"I'm fed up telling them,

Never take a suite off a stranger"!!!

'Road Accident Excuses'

'I was sure the old fellow would never make it to the other side of the road, so, I struck him with my car'.

'In The Dark'

During a recent football match of which I was engaged on duty within the stadium.

I was standing at the touchline, near to the players tunnel, when the 'floodlighting' system went out, placing the entire stadium in darkness.

The referee immediately summoned all the players, on both sides, to the centre circle and began to lead them off the park.

As the players filtered off towards the dressing room. The referee and his assistants were just about to enter the 'players tunnel' area, when a spectator, among the crowd shouted,

"This shouldn't make any difference to you Ref, you've been in the dark all bloody night!!

'Wood U Beleeve It?'

Whilst checking our 'Missing Person' reports at the office, I was looking up a recent report involving a young girl, when I noticed an update from a young officer, which stated,

"Her mother is unable to give any further information as she is dyslexic and cannot read or right"…!!

"Neither could the 'writter' updating this resort"!

'What's Perjury'

During a trial within the Glasgow Sheriff Court. A witness was called to give evidence for the defence.

The accused in the 'dock' just happened to be a very good friend of the witness and when questioned by the Procurator Fiscal, he became very evasive and flippant, in his answers.
The Procurator Fiscal, who was by this time, becoming annoyed and fed up with the witness and his lack of genuine response to his questions, said to him,

"Let me remind you, that you took an oath, to tell the truth, the whole truth and nothing but the truth"!

The witness replied indignantly,

"I am well aware of that sir"!

"Well", said the Procurator Fiscal,
"Are you well aware of what you can get for perjury"?

As quick as a flash, the witness replied,

"Aye, about £20,000 a year, if you're a polis"!

'Road Accident Excuses'

'Coming home, I drove into the wrong house and collided with a tree I don't have in my driveway'.

'Hello Dolly'

One day while I was engaged in uniform Police duties within the office, I had occasion to answer the telephone to a Chief Inspector from the Discipline Department, requesting to speak with another police officer, who was within the office.

The officer concerned was always playing practical jokes on the younger members within the office and would 'boast' about what he had done to them.

With this in mind and eager to reverse the roll on him for showing off.

I pressed the 'mute' button on the desk telephone and summoned the 'boaster' concerned, aptly named, 'Gattling Gub'.
I then informed him, that it was his wife calling for him!

I then released the 'mute' button as he snatched the telephone from my hand and promptly blurted out.

"Hello doll, what can I do for you"?

To which the Chief Inspector replied,

"Well, you can refer to me as sir for a start"!!

As for me, I got great satisfaction from his 'body language' as I watched him with telephone in one hand, squirm to attention!

'D.N.A. Not Required'

A senior cop receives a call to attend a suspicious death within an 'Ice-cream cafe'.

Accompanied by a young raw recruit, he makes his way to the location.

On arrival, they walk into the café and are shown by the proprietor to the body.

The senior cop turns to the young recruit and says,

"Right, have a look and tell me what you see"

The young cop bends down, looks and says,

"His legs, from his feet to his hips, are covered in ice-cream"!

"Okay"! Says the senior cop. "Have another good look".

The young cop bends down again to look.

"From his waist to his shoulders, he's covered in a sticky 'raspberry sauce'!

"Good". Says the senior cop.
"Now, have one more thorough look and tell me if you know the cause of death".

He bends down for a third time, studies the body, then stands up and says, "His head is covered with flaked chocolate"!

"So what does that tell you then"? Asks the senior cop.

"Simple", replied the young officer.

"He 'topped' himself"!!

'Crime Doesn't Always Pay'

A would be thief, entered a well-established clothing store and after perusing the clothing rails for several minutes, he picked out a pair of trousers that appeared to take his fancy.

Dressed in an old pair of denim jeans, he asked the assistant to direct him to the changing room, to try them on.

As the store was relatively busy, the assistant couldn't remain with him and left to tend to another customer.

However, when the assistant returned a short time later, the male had eloped with the trousers, leaving behind his old denim jeans.

Having been duped by the thief, the manager was about to mark it down to another theft for statistics, when he noticed a slight bulge in the back pocket of the jeans.

It turned out to be a leather wallet, which contained £65.00 in cash.

The loss became a profit as the trousers had a price tag of only £24.99.

This was one thief, who learned the hard way that crime doesn't pay and at this rate, it wouldn't be long before he became 'bankrupt'!!

"THE ADVENTURES OF PC ARCHiE BAULD"

BY 'SEAMOR TOONS'

'Who Was That?'

Whilst working within the police motor vehicle garage at the start of my traffic patrol officer career, I was being shown all the various parts of a car engine, what can go wrong and how to repair it.

Later, I was walking down to the end of the garage, when the wall telephone started ringing.

The garage Sergeant shouted for me to answer it, so I went over and picked it up and the following is what took place.

"Helen Street Police Garage, can I help you"?

"Yes you can", replied the caller. "You can tell me what is happening with the nightshift Superintendent's car"?

"I have absolutely no idea what's happening"! I replied.

To which the caller responded, "Do you know who you are speaking too"?

"No"! I replied. "Should I"?

"Well, this is Superintendent McKinlay"! He said.

"And do you know who you're speaking to"? I said rather indignantly!

"No I don't", he answered.

Which I replied, "Good"! And promptly put the telephone down.

"Who was that"? Enquired the garage Sergeant.

"Wrong number"! I said, as I quickly walked off.

'Lost for Words'

One day out on the Main Street of the area I worked, a 'bus driver' friend of my brothers approached me.
I remarked about how 'bronze' tanned he was and he said he was just back from a family holiday.
He then said that while away on holiday, he had lost his father.
Not realising what he meant, I said,

"Don't tell me, a pub crawl, I'm the same, it's that cheap foreign plonk, it gives me the 'Tex Ritters' ....

At this point he interrupted me and said,

"No Harry, when I say I lost him, I mean, he died...."! Oops!!

'Smoking Cough'

During a Social night out at the Police Club, I was sitting at a table opposite another couple.
Later the same evening, the woman began to cough and splutter.
This went on for several minutes, with the coughing becoming more intense, as the woman's face changed colour and as I looked over at her, she appeared to be choking and unable to draw a breath.

I quickly left my seat and ran over to assist her, "Watch"! I said.
Grabbing hold of her head, I promptly pushed it down between her legs.
Suddenly, she stopped coughing and began screaming and howling hysterically, in serious distress.

'How was I to know she had a 'lit' cigarette in her mouth'?

'The Job's Fucked'

A regular saying within the Police Force was, 'The Job's Fucked' from the many disgruntled City of Glasgow Police Officers in the early seventies.
Every other week, a Police Officer, using the all systems radio airways, would interrupt the occasional silence, by broadcasting to all mobile and radio stations, 'The Job's Fucked'!

One particular day, an Assistant Chief Constable of the Police Force was within the Headquarters Radio Control Room, when over the radio came the aforesaid,

"The Job's Fucked"!

The Assistant Chief Constable in attendance, on hearing this announcement, immediately picked up the radio handset and broadcasted a response,

"Would the station who just transmitted that statement, please identify yourself"?

The same voice replied, "What for"? "The Job's Fucked"!

Getting frustrated by this anonymous callers remarks on air, the Assistant Chief Constable again broadcasted, but this time, he identified himself over the radio.

"This is Assistant Chief Constable Bennie, so would the officer transmitting that statement, please identify yourself to me"?

To which the caller paused for a moment before replying in a drawl voice,

"It's no' that fucked"!!

'Now That's Magic'

One evening, along with my partner Ewan Cameron, I was on mobile patrol, when I stopped a car for having a rear tail-light out.

I informed the driver why I had stopped him and he got out of his car and went to the rear to check for himself.

While doing this, Cameron walked to the front of the car to check for any other obvious defects.

The driver, meantime, on seeing the defective rear light, lifted his foot and 'kicked' the light cover a few times, at which point, due to faulty wiring, the light came back on.

He then looked at me with a smug grin on his face and said,

"There ye go, as if by magic! It just needed a wee kick in the right place"!

At which point Cameron said,

"Good for you mate, now, would you like to try that 'trick' on your windscreen and see if you can get a tax disc to appear.

Now, that would be magic"!!

'Road Accident Excuses'

'A truck reversed through my windscreen into my wife's face'.

'Who's a Boot?'

I was contacted one day to return to the office for an urgent escort duty.

On my arrival back at the office, the Sergeant, instructed me to take a CID car and drive over to the Police Headquarters and uplift a policewoman called Delia Blain, to accompany me, with the transport of a female prisoner.

I arrived at Police Headquarters and walked into the front office, where I enquired from the Police control room staff, in my broadest Glaswegian accent, "Is Delia aboot"?

To which one of the cops replied,

"No she is not, in fact, she's quite a nice girl"!!

'Control Room Story'

When I was a motorcycle cop, I received the following call from the Control Room.

"A.S. Control calls Tango Charlie One Four, to attend and assist in the removal of a stolen Suzuki motorcycle, recovered, abandoned in Queen Street, Glasgow.
Please note, there is a police woman standing by it".

I then enquired from the Controller,

"Tango Charlie One Four, is it rideable"?

To which the Controller replied, "Affirmative Tango Charlie One Four and she's not bad looking either"!!

'Straight from the Horse'

During a drugs trial in Glasgow, a Senior Detective Officer, was cited as an expert witness, to clarify that the amount of drugs found on an accused person, was being used to supply drug 'deals' and not, as the Defence claimed, for his personal use.

The Defence agent continued to press the point that the drugs were for his clients' own personal use.

The Senior Detective Officer however, in his role as an expert witness for the Crown, was re-iterating his response, that when 'cut' into equal quantities, it was a clear indication, it was for supplying drug 'deals'.
The Detective continued, that if it were for personal use, there would be no need to 'cut' or divide it into equal parts.

However, the Defence agent persisted with his client's futile excuse about personal use and pursued this line of questioning.
Finally, the Sheriff, bored by this continual line of questioning, interrupted the Defence agent and in a stern voice asked,

"Excuse me Mr Corr, but, have you ever been charged with cruelty to animals"?

The Defence agent, looked up at the Sheriff on the bench and with a puzzled expression asked the Sheriff,

"Why M'Lord"?

To which the Sheriff responded,

"Because you're flogging a dead horse, now let's move on"!!

'Kiss Me Quick'

In 1976, during the Police International Tattoo, being held within the Kelvin Hall Arena, in Glasgow.
I was performing a routine display with the rest of the Motorcycle Section.

However, prior to our performance, we had to take turns on the Police Motorcycle stand and answer questions from the members of the public attending, as well as giving their children accompanying them, a seat on the Police motorbike, or in a traffic patrol car.

Afterwards, when I was on the stand taking my turn, a young female, civilian staff member of the Traffic Police Administration Department entered the stand.

On seeing her, I put my arms around her and took her in a passionate embrace, leaning her over the motorcycle saddle and proceeded to give her a long, deep, sensual kiss. (As a joke).

As we straightened up again, I noticed, she had a stunned expression on her face and was blushing uncontrollably.
For a moment, I thought I had 'swooned' her off her feet, but to my total embarrassment and total humiliation, she said,

"Harry, I'd like you to meet my dad and my brother"!

I turned around to see two men of six feet in height, glaring at me!

'Road Accident Excuses'

'In an attempt to kill a fly, I drove into a telephone pole'

'The Battery Store'

Out one day on patrol, my partner 'Kenny' was telling me his car battery was 'flat' and he wanted to go along to the Police Garage in Helen Street, to 'charge' it up.
When we arrived, Kenny went to see 'Alex', the 'Garage Sergeant' and asked for his permission to 'charge' his car battery.

Alex said, "Yeah, on you go, but d'you know how to do it"?

Kenny replied confidently, "No problem, I've seen the set up"!

Off he went, carrying his car battery along to the 'Battery Store'.
On entering the 'store', there must have been about thirty-to-forty large car batteries, all 'connected' up to each other and all being 'charged' at the same time.
While I looked around at the complicated system, linking all the batteries together, Kenny lifted his battery up into a space on the shelf.
He then, took the 'positive' and 'negative' wire leads and connected the 'negative' lead to the battery beside his and then took the 'positive' and 'clipped' it onto his battery.......

'Bang'! The battery next to his exploded and within seconds, there was a chain reaction, 'Bang'! 'Bang'! 'Bang'!
As the entire 'battery' store resembled the 'Fourth of July'!

Three and four at a time, every battery in the store was 'exploding' 'round about us, as we were showered in 'acid' and bits off the 'exploding' batteries!

I quickly did a runner, leaving big 'Kenny' with a 'helluva' job to do in explaining his obvious serious mistake to 'Alex'!

'I'll Tell Him Tomorrow, Maybe'!

One evening, a well-dressed male accountant, picked up a young female prostitute from the 'red' light district of Blythswood Square in Glasgow.
Having agreed a price for sex, he drove off with her in his car, to her home address, on the Southside of the City.

They both stripped off and engaged in sexual intercourse, after which, the accountant got dressed and quickly left the house, while the female was in the toilet washing and failing to pay the prostitute the agreed fee for the services she had provided.

Not to be outdone so easily, the aggrieved female contacted her 'minder', who just happened to be in the nearby vicinity.
Armed with a 'baseball bat', he confronted the accountant as he made his way out of the high flat tower block en-route to his parked car.

The accountant, displayed some wonderful athleticism skills and 'Ran like Hell', pursued by 'Babe Ruth', the armed baseballer.

At this point, an anonymous call was made to the Police Office, regarding, one male being pursued by another male, armed with a large 'club'.
A police car was immediately dispatched, to attend the call, whereby, on their arrival, they quickly apprehended 'Babe Ruth', handcuffed him and placed him in the rear of the police car, while they obtained a full statement from the 'shaken' accountant.

Whilst noting the statement, one of the officers was beckoned over by a female in the large assembled crowd.

It was the young prostitute who had been involved.

She then related to the police officer her side of the story, with regards to the events that had taken place earlier.

Armed with this new information, the officer returned to the accountant, who blurted out,

"Whatever she said, she's lying, she's a lying little whore"!

The officer then related her story, as told to him.

The 'smug' accountant then freely admitted giving her a lift home because she looked unwell, but strenuously denied being involved with her in any sexual act, infact, he went as far to say,

"I did not have sexual relations with that woman".
(Where have I heard that line before Bill?)

"She's a lying little whore, but then, what do you expect from the residents of this area"? He replied rather indignantly.

The officer then said, facetiously,

"You're right enough sir, who ever heard of an Accountant cheating you out of your money"?

The officer then paused for a moment before continuing,

"Anyway sir, you definitely deny having had sexual intercourse with her"?

"I certainly do! What do you take me for, I'm a happily married man"? He responded with his pitiful denial.

"Well sir"! Said the officer. "I'm so glad to hear you say that, because apparently, she's been diagnosed 'H.I.V. positive' and she continues to entertain men in her flat for unprotected sexual intercourse"!

On hearing this, the accountant's facial expression changed, as the colour visibly drained rapidly from his face.

"Are you okay sir"? Asked the officer. "You look like a ghost"!

The accountant replied very quietly,

"Not really! I'm feeling a bit nausea and would just like to go home to my wife and my family now"!

"But what about 'Babe Ruth' with the baseball bat, we haven't charged him yet"? Said the officer.

The accountant replied,

"I'd like to drop all the charges against him and go home please, I'm feeling very ill with all this"!

"I'm not surprised sir, but are you sure, because he looks very nasty with that big baseball bat"? Said the condescending officer.

"Yes I'm sure, now can I just go home please? I've wasted enough time here". He said.

"Not a problem sir, just sign my notebook to the effect, you don't want to proceed with the charges"! Said the officer. "No harm done, so by all means, you can go on your way"!

The accountant then walked off rather unsteadily to his car before driving off.

The first officer then said to the second officer.

"You might have told him you were only kidding about the H.I.V."!

To which the first officer replied,

"What for"? "You heard him give the 'Bill Clinton' speech",

"I did not have sexual relations with that woman"!

"Now why would I disbelieve the lying, cheating bastard"!!

P.S. If you're the accountant involved and reading this.

It was only a joke!

'**A Secret Service**'

This is a story I just had to include.
It has nothing to do with the police, but refers to my son Scott, who was six years old at the time and was fascinated with his super hero, 'James Bond'.

One Sunday afternoon, having attended the church in the morning, we were relaxing within our house, when the telephone rang.

Quick as a flash, my son Scott answered,

"Hello, James Bond here"!

The person at the other end of the telephone paused for a moment, then said,

"Is that you Scott"?

Slightly puzzled by the caller, Scott answered 'Yes'!

"Do you know who this is"? Enquired the caller.

Still puzzled, Scott replied, "No"!

The caller responded by saying,

"Well I spoke to you this morning in church! Now do you know who it is"?

Scott paused for a moment, then replied,

"Is it you God"?

He was nearly right. It was the Minister!

'Wanted'

Several years ago, my oldest daughter Samantha, who would be about five or six at the time, was out playing in the front garden, when a car drove past at speed and the driver stuck his tongue out at her.

This really upset her and she ran into the house to tell me. I listened to her intently and then said I would look out for him when I was out on Police patrol and deal with him severely.
My daughter was delighted with this response from her policeman dad.

Next day, she returned from school, "That's him Dad"! She said.
Handing me this sketch of the 'suspect' responsible for sticking his tongue out at her, for me to hand out to my colleagues.

'WANTED'

As you can see from her excellent artistic sketch, he is instantly recognisable and extremely......Da...Da... Da... Damn ugly!!

'Ladies and Gents, No Bother'

Several years ago, the shift I was working on, organised a day out with all of our kids at a local swimming club.

I shared a locker with my young son and my two daughters aged ten and five years did likewise.
Later, after we had left the pool and had a shower, my two daughters were drying themselves, when the youngest one, Kimmy, decided to go to the toilet.

Out she went from the shared cubicle, only to return several minutes later to ask her older sister,

"Samantha, am I a male or a female"?

'Bad Breath'

The morning after a 'heavy' night out, where everybody who was present, had gorged him or herself with food and drank the pub dry of all alcohol.
A certain C.I.D. officer, called into the Police Office for a cup of coffee and a quick cure for a severe 'hangover'.

As he approached me, he said,

"Harry, can I have a cup of your coffee to make me feel better"?

To which I replied,

"On one condition Bob"! "You could go outside and eat a dogs 'turd' and tone your breath down a bit"!!

"Now that would make me feel better"!!

'Yuill and Dodds'

This poem was written during the mineworkers strike, April 1984.

Yuill and Dodds (Haulage) were contracted to play a big part and were escorted to and from Ravenscraig and Hunterston, when fully laden, in convoy, by uniform police car and motorcycle patrols.

'Money for Old Coke'

I love my Morris minor though it's 25 years old
I take it out on Sundays if the weather's not too cold.

We took it out on Sunday last the wife, the weans and me
And drove along the Fenwick Moor for a picnic by the sea.

We admired the lovely countryside truly the work of Gods
When thundering around a corner came a fucking 'Yuill and Dodds'!!

As it trundled up towards us, it's size just grew and grew
I had visions of having 'Scania' stamped across my brew.

As the lorry thundered past me I thought my life had 'endit'!
Wait till I get my hands on him that trucking 'Mexican Bandit'.

The coal dust was just clearing from the 'bandits' little ploy
When coming straight towards me was the 'Ravenscraig' convoy.

Now 'Yuill and Dodds' are well renowned from here to 'Timbuctoo'

The Polis were always stopping them for things they shouldn't do.

But now the tables are all turned they are 'BUDDIES' everyone
A Polis car goes out in front and leads them on their run.

Now the miners aren't very pleased the way they drive a truck
None of them will ever stop 'cause they just don't give a 'fuck'.

The drivers now are all caged in I don't know how they stick it
But I hear they're on a 'bonus' if they 'hit and run' a 'picket'.

'Yuill and Dodds' will run forever I hear the people say
And when the miners realise this perhaps they'll call it a day.

So come on boys, throw in the towel and let's just see it 'endit'
We've been counting up our money and now we'd like to spend it.

(Many police officers disagreed with the apparent taking of sides in this 'political' dispute and also the views of miners leader 'Arthur Scargill')

Single White Male'

A young 'ginger' haired, 'spotty' faced Police recruit called in at his local 'Asda' Foodstore.
As he got to the 'checkout', he placed a loaf of bread, a pint of milk and a can of beans on the conveyor belt.
The pretty female cashier, looked up at him, as she began 'scanning' his goods.

"Are you single"? She asked him.

"Yeah"! He replied. "How did you know"?

To which the pretty cashier replied,

"Cause you're an ugly bastard"!

129

'No Profit in Theft'

A man walked into a shop and placed a £20.00 note on the counter.
He then asked the female assistant for change of the note.

The cashier duly obliged and opened the cash drawer.
Quick as a flash, the man put his hand into the till and grabbed what monies he could before running off out of the shop into the street, leaving behind the £20.00 note, he had placed on the counter.
On checking the contents of the shop cash register, it was discovered the thief had snatched the total sum of ..£14.00.
Thereby, making the thief a loss of £6.00 and the shopkeeper a profit of £6.00.
This is one robber, who would be well advised to start going straight and work for a living!

'Toilet Paper'

It's amazing how they now talk about re-cycling refuse.
Way back in the 50s and 60s everybody in the street where I live did it. It was called in those days as, 'Nae Lavvy Paper'!

None of your 'Velvet Andrex', 'Soft Tissue', 'Quilted', or any other 'crap' for us, pardon the pun! That wee 'Labrador' dog wasn't even born then.
Now, if you were posh and could afford it, you used 'Izal'!
It's slippery surface didn't wipe your arse, it just spread it further than 'Flora' margarine. No wonder they wrote, 'Now Wash Hands Please'!
As for my family, it was the Daily Record cut into neat squares!
However, it was the Glasgow Herald for any visitors! Pure Class!

'Everything is Free'

One day in the office, we were in the process of organising a 'night out' for the entire shift to attend.
We were all 'chipping' in with various venues to contact and arrange our 'doo'!
Some were saying it was too expensive for drink or the food they served wasn't very good and there was a severe lack of 'burds'.
When out of the 'blue', Andy Kouskous, the Shift Sergeant piped up,

"We could go to that new place that has opened up in Hamilton"!

"Do you know if it's good grub and cheap booze"? Asked Jim.

"What's the talent like"? Enquired Big Alan.

"Well", said Andy, "Apparently, you get supplied with free cigarettes all night",

"You get 'free' drink, bought for you all night and the food menu is available for you to eat what you want, when you want and that's also absolutely free"!!

"But, this is the best bit, at the end of the night, you can get as much sex as you want"!

The guys are all 'dumfounded' with this news, then, one of them, slightly puzzled by this offer, asks,

"Who exactly told you all this Andy"?

To which Andy proudly replied, "My sister"!!!

'Three in a Bed'

Fed up with the many 'Men Only' nights that their respective Police husbands and boyfriends were having, the 'partners' decided it was their turn to have a 'ladies night'.

One of the wives took charge of organising it for them and had a video selection leaflet from her local video rental shop. In it, she had noticed a certain video title called, 'Three In A Bed' and having discussed it with some of the other wives and partners, they unanimously agreed, this was the video for their 'blue ladies night'.

With a time and date agreed by all concerned, they arranged to meet at the home of the wife responsible for organising the video. They also agreed that everyone attending the 'blue' night video show should supply their own particular brand of alcohol for the occasion.

The big 'night' duly arrived and all the excited ladies had assembled within the designated house.
They eagerly passed the video around with the title, 'Three In A Bed', boldly displayed for all to see.

Was it two women and one man or two men and one woman?
Their imagination was running wild and they couldn't wait to find out!
All eyes were on the operator as she stooped over to insert the video, there was a moment of sheer anticipation from the excited ladies.
As they focused on the screen, a huge 'sigh' of disappointed rang around the room, as up on the screen before their very eyes, came the title, 'Three In A Bed' starring,

Former World Champions, 'Jocky Wilson', 'Eric Bristow' and 'Phil 'The Power' Taylor', they had picked up an exhibition darts video!!

None of your sixty nines '69' here, but there was plenty of ... 'one hundred and eighty'!

'Barbers'

A Police Officer walks into a 'barbers' and asks for a 'haircut and a shave'!

The barber cuts his hair and then begins to 'shave' him. As he does, he 'nicks' him with the razor.

"Your face is familiar, have I shaved you before"? The barber asks.

"Yes", replied the cop. "But it's healed up since then"!

'Canteen'

A cop walks into the Police canteen and is approached by the counter assistant Cathy who says,

"I have braised kidneys, boiled tongue, fried liver and pigs feet"!

The cop replies,

"Don't tell me your health problems Cathy, just give me something to eat"!

'Football Detail'

One evening, the Traffic Department were all reporting for 'football detail', which is when a big Sporting Football event is taking place in Glasgow.

Before, during and after the match, we all have specific duties to perform.

Having been instructed my duties, my partner Jimmy McNulty and I went out on our specific patrol area.

Whilst driving along a road, near to the stadium, with parked cars lining either side of the well-illuminated roadway, I saw a 'sports' type car coming towards us, from the opposite direction.

Jimmy, who was driving the police car at the time, began to move more and more into the centre of the road, in order to restrict the space of the oncoming vehicle.

Due to this action, the opposing driver was forced to stop.

Jimmy then, drove alongside, to the driver's window and enquired from him, if he was in a hurry.

The driver replied that he was, as he was on his way to work.

Jimmy then said,

"Well you'll save some time when you get there. You won't need to switch off your car lights".

Then, as Jimmy started to drive off, he remarked just loud enough for the driver to hear, "You wanker"!

The driver, looking at his dashboard to see why his lights were not on, then suddenly realised what Jimmy had just called him.

At that point, he leant out of his car window and shouted after us,

"I'll wank you"!

To which Jimmy shouted back,

"Not tonight darling, I'm on the football detail"!!!

'Licenced To Bleed'

On another occasion with Jimmy, we stopped a car for failing to comply with a 'red light' and driving through the junction.

We immediately pursued and stopped the male offender.

As was normal, Jimmy spoke with the driver, checking his details etc, while I walked around the vehicle looking for any obvious defects.

As I got to the front of the vehicle, I saw Jimmy punch the driver in the face and as the driver threw himself back onto the passenger seat, Jimmy then tried to go through his open window, to get at him.
I quickly grabbed Jimmy around the waist and pulled him away, whilst he protested vigorously about the drivers' actions.

I managed to calm Jimmy down, (if that is possible) and get him to sit in the police car, where he explained to me the following.

It seems that when Jimmy asked the driver to produce his wee red book Driving licence, the driver had turned away for a moment, before producing a licence containing 2 x £1.00 notes inside.

Jimmy enquired what the money in his licence was for and the driver, out with my view and hearing said, "It's yours, take it"!
This attempt at 'bribery' completely 'flipped' Jimmy into action.

As it was, Jimmy sent the driver away looking like something from 'Comic Relief', with a real 'bloody' red nose for his bother!

Mind you. With wee Jimmy, the 'Red Nose' was donated completely 'free' of any 'charge'!

'Roast Chicken and Chips'

I think all the resident 'nut cases' in the areas I worked, waited until I was performing nightshift duty, so they could pay me a visit at the Police Office and obtain free counseling sessions, followed by a cigarette, a cup of tea and a chocolate biscuit.

At one point, I was performing that many counseling sessions, I thought I was employed with the N.H.S.

One of my many regular visitors was a larger than life female called Georgina Hill, or 'Georgie', as she preferred to be called.

Georgie was a big woman in every sense of the word and I would describe her as a female, not blessed with the best of looks and when she put her make up on, she had a face like a 'Halloween' cake. Obviously a lack of mirrors in the house.

She was excessively overweight by several 'stones' and with her 'womanly' body shape stuffed into a 'tweed' coat that was too small for her, she resembled a 'burst sofa'!

Now that I have dispersed with the pleasantries, I will relate my story to you.

The office door opened just after midnight and in walked Georgie, larger than life.

"Hello Mister Morris, just 'popped' in to see how you are and have a wee blether with you"! She said.

"I'm fine thanks Georgie, what about yourself. I haven't seen you around for a few weeks"? I enquired.

That was my first big mistake of the night! It was the cue for Georgie to relate to me her entire Medical history, pausing only to catch a breath!

"Well, I don't think I told you, but, I've been in Hospital. I was suffering from a bit of woman trouble"!

She then proceeded to do a 'Les Dawson' and 'Roy Barraclough' female impersonation, followed by a 'mime' artist expression as she pointed to her 'fat belly'!

"All oot"! "All oot"! She said. As she made hand signs across her stomach like she was a paid up member of the Masonic Lodge.

Her voice becoming quieter and her actions more animated, the more serious her operation sounded.

"Anyway"! She continued, "The surgeon opened me up, right across my stomach and done the business, I was that wide open, they had to call in an upholsterer to staple my wound together".

The nurses said, "Georgie, what a mess you were in hen! That was major woman problems you had"!

"D'you know Harry, see efter that operation, I was bloody 'ravishing', I could've eaten a 'scabby cat' 'atween two slice of stale bread"!

I interrupted her. "I think you mean ravenous, Georgie"!

"Same thing Harry"! She said dismissively. "Anyway, the Staff Nurse said",

"I'm sorry Georgie, but ye canny eat, you'll need to wait for the Doctor to come 'round first"!

Then they started all the small talk with me, like,

"Have you got any kids Georgie"? And "Are they boys or lassies"?

"Well 'bugger me'! Pardon my expression, but by this time, my stomach thinks that my throats been cut in the operation and all they can talk aboot is kids!
Now, don't get me wrong Harry, I love kids and right at that moment I could probably have eaten a whole wan tae myself"!

"But in fact, right now, all I'm thinking about, is 'Colonel Sanders' Kentucky Fried Chicken ..... I'll even pluck the thing myself"!

"Anyways"!   "Next thing is, the nurse tells me they have a special surprise for me"!

"What is it I'm thinking to myself"?
"Has the Surgeon removed the wrong orgasms"?
"Has he lost his 'Rolex' watch"?
"Or maybe they've found bits of 'Shergar', 'cause that butcher in the Main Street is definitely 'Dodgy', or maybe he just fancies me"!

"Gonny put me oot my bloody misery and tell me"? I said to them.

They both looked at each other for a moment, then the Staff Nurse said,

"Right, after you've had a nice hot bath, I've arranged for the kitchen staff to make your favourite meal, 'Roast Chicken and Chips', just for you"!

"Oh ya wee dancer"! I said. "I hope it's the size of an Ostrich, 'cause I'm feeling pure anorexic"!

Well, you never seen anybody get in and oot a bath as quick as me and when a looked at my old 'Jean Brody', with all they staples across it, I resembled a centre page, of 'wan' 'o my weans school jotters!

It was the first time I had seen myself in a full length mirror and my big 'Jazz Drum' was sticking oot, like a 'Pigeon's' landing board!
I kid you not, you could've balanced a tray o' drinks on my erse!

Anyway, I'm diverting again"! "However, I'm oot the bath and I'm drying myself and just as I lifted my left leg up tae dry my feet and Guess whit"?

She then performed her 'Les Dawson' impression again and said,

"Some o' the staples started popping and I thought I was gonny 'burst' oot all over the floor.

(God forbid! ... That's me thinking to myself!)

A shouted for the nurses, but it was really another upholsterer I needed.
The nurses came rushing in and whisked me away, I had to get emergency treatment".

"Well, they put me on a 'drip' and gave me an emergency blood transmission to replace what I had lost"!

"As if that wasn't enough, the nurse then tells me",

"I'm sorry Georgie, but you can't have anything to eat"!

I said, "Whit! Are you yanking my chain? I've had that 'Nil by Mouth' sign up on my bed that long, my family think that's my real name in French"!

Just at that the Auxiliary nurse comes over to me and asks,

"Do you need a bed pan Georgie"?

"Are you trying to take the piss"? I said sarcastically.
"You need to eat, before you can excrete"!

I then turned my attention back to the nurse and said,

"And who is going to get my 'Roast Chicken and Chips' then"?

"The bin"! She replied. "They cook threw it out"!

"Now, as she put her arm across to tidy my bed sheet, I thought about biting it aff"!

(Just at that point, there was a noise and the rear door of the Police Office was opened and I could hear my Police colleagues coming in for their tea break.)

Interrupting Georgie in full flow, I said,

"Well Georgie, I could sit and listen to you going through your Medical History all night, but I'll need to interrupt you, because that's the boys in the Police 'Panda' arriving for their refreshment period and you'll never guess what I'm going to have for my dinner"?

She stared at me for a moment, before a smile broke out across her face and she said in an excited voice,

"Roast Chicken and Chips"!

To which I replied,

"No"! "Three quarters of an hour like everybody else"!!

"Goodnight Georgie"!

'Cobblers'

A prisoner is released after serving twenty-five years in prison.

As he goes through his property, he finds a receipt in his jacket pocket for a 'Cobblers'.
He goes to the repair shop and handed it over to the Cobbler, who studies it carefully.

"A pair of brown brogues, to be 'soled and healed'? He asked.

"Yeah, that's correct"! Said the prisoner.

"Be ready, Friday"! Said the Cobbler.

'Forensic Psychologist'

A case at the High Court in Glasgow, involved a 'Carer', looking after clients with 'Learning Disabilities'. It was alleged, this particular 'Carer' was taking some of them into a secured room, where he showed them 'Pornographic Videos', it was further alleged that he had also sexually abused some of them'!

Unable to understand the procedures of the Court, the witness / complainers had to be taken in separately, prior to the Court sitting to let them see the inside of the courtroom. The Judge also made himself available, in order to meet with them and ask them a few simple questions, in order to confirm, if they new the difference between what is the 'Truth' and what is a 'Lie'!

Having satisfied the various 'wigs' present within the Court, that they new what the obvious difference was, the case for the Prosecution commenced.

During the evidence, a major part of the case relied on the evidence of experts, in this case, Forensic Psychologists, who had interviewed the witnesses and the Defence Forensic Psychologist, who studied the resultant copy report.

It was during the Defence evidence that the Forensic Psychologist employed by them as their expert witness, identified herself to the court, citing her list of rather impressive qualifications.
Her evidence was critical of the Prosecution Psychologist Report and the method that was used by them, in obtaining their subsequent 'damning' results.

The main objection being, that the Prosecution Forensic Psychologist had occasion to repeat some of the questions being put to the victims, during the expert examination.

Out of twelve questions asked, to each victim, at least eight questions, required to be repeated.

Thereby, in her expert opinion, by repeating the question to the victims, it prompted a totally different answer.

She also stated, due to this method used by the Prosecution, each of the victims allegedly abused had been 'scaled' higher in their 'mental ability' and 'understanding' than they should have been!

The Advocate Depute, representing the Prosecution then stood up and began the cross-examination of the Defence Expert Witness.

Several moments passed, whereby the Prosecution asked some questions. It was noticeable, when she did, she turned her head away and looked toward the jury at the opposite side of the courtroom each time, thereby, not addressing her questions directly at the Defence Witness.

I also observed that the Advocate Depute did not ask her initial question in her forthright clear voice, but did so when repeating the question and whilst directly facing the Defence witness full on.

At this point it became obviously clear to my colleagues and I present within the court that she was deliberately doing this, in order to prompt the Defence Witness into having to ask her to repeat the question.

Suddenly, the Advocate Depute stopped her specific line of enquiry and staring directly at the Defence Witness, she asked her to confirm again for the Court her Expert Qualifications.

"I'm a Forensic Psychologist, a Clinical Psychologist, a Member of The Fellowship of Psychology, Etc, Etc, Etc…"!

"Thank you for reminding the Court of your very impressive array of expert qualifications Doctor, most impressive indeed"!

"Now! Could you please tell the Court how you would 'scale' your individual performance in the question and answer session we have just completed, taking into consideration, I've asked you several relevant questions similar to those, asked of the witnesses, with notable 'Learning Disabilities' by the Crown Prosecution Expert Psychologist and out of the ten asked of you, I've had to repeat at least seven of them"?

"Now Doctor, having previously stated your qualifications to the Court, it is obvious, you don't possess a 'Learning Disability', to submit, as an obvious excuse for not understanding my specific, but simple line of questions, first time around"!

The Doctor tried to qualify her responses,

"But I did not hear your questions clearly, so therefore I had difficulty in understanding them properly"! She said.

The Advocate Depute, paused for a second, while focusing on the Defence Expert, Forensic Psychologist and her pathetic excuse in response, then replied,

"Exactly Doctor! Therefore when you asked me to repeat the question, it was to understand it and not to prompt you to give me a different answer"!

Then turning to address the assembled jury, knowing she a 'scored' with her cross examination, she said,

"I have no more questions for this expert witness"!

Before returning to her seat in the court.

It was a pleasure to be present during some excellent expert and extremely clever questioning by the 'Crown' Prosecution!

That was a great Court case!

'Dr Whyte at your Disposal'

Whilst on duty one night within the office, the front door burst open and in ran a male in his mid twenties, who was a known trouble maker in the area.
He was bleeding profusely, from a large deep laceration to his chin. Commonly referred to as a 'Kirk Douglas'!

He was screaming frantically,

"Help me, I'm getting chased wi' a team and their 'tooled' up wi' blades"!

I then heard a loud disturbance outside and as I looked up, I saw about eight youths, staring down from the pedestrian walkway above, armed with knives and clubs.

On seeing me lift the radio to call for assistance, they all ran off.

My next priority was to try and stem the 'bleeding' from his serious facial injury and summon an ambulance to attend.

Using paper towels and applying pressure to the wound, I was able to stem the flow of blood, while I searched through the office First Aid Kit, but, the items contained inside, were so old, they would not be out of place on the 'Antique Roadshow'!
The sterile pads would've given him 'gangrene'!!

At this point I noticed on the wall of the female officers toilet, a 'Dr Whyte Sanitary Towel' machine.
Now they're most definitely sterile!!

Out of the sight of my young 'hard man' victim, I quickly ripped open the small package and removed the 'sanitary towel', which was about four inches in length, with a 'hoop' at either end.

Removing the sodden bloodstained paper towels from his face, I replaced them with the sanitary towel, covering the wound and looped the 'hoops' on either end, over his ears, to hold it in place.

(Why hoops, I'll never know? But I'll accept explanations on a stamped address envelope. From women only!)

I then told him to apply pressure to it.

He sat quietly, awaiting the arrival of the ambulance, totally unaware of what the sterile dressing on his chin was.
That was however, until four of my police colleagues arrived at the office, in response to my call for assistance.

They all instantly recognised the victim, who was sitting quietly feeling sorry for himself, with his 'hammock' dressing dangling from his ears.

That was it they just couldn't contain themselves as they all fell about laughing and making trivial excuses to the victim, in order to leave the office.

A few minutes later, the ambulance arrived and after a few 'titters' of laughter from the paramedic crew, they soon removed the injured male, complete with 'sanitary' towel, to the local accident and emergency hospital.

After they had left, as you would imagine, there was the usual 'period' of sick jokes from the cops who were present.

Particularly, as this was the beginning of the 'festive period'.

"THE ADVENTURES OF PC ARCHiE BAULD"

BY 'SEAMOR TOONS'

146

'Sick Joke'

Whilst on motorcycle patrol duties, I was involved in a road accident.
A big orange and green Corporation double-decked bus, in the City Centre of Glasgow, collided with me, head on.

(Don't laugh, that bit was true)!

Anyway, I was knocked unconscious and rushed by ambulance to the accident and emergency, where I was admitted to an observation ward.

Several hours later, I regained consciousness and tried to focus my eyes.

I looked to my right and 'John Wayne' appeared to be in the hospital bed next to me.

I then looked to my left and 'Clint Eastwood' was in the other one.

Rubbing my eyes frantically, I called for the nurse and said,

"Where am I"? "Where am I"?

To which the nurse replied,

"You're in the Western"!! (Infirmary)

'No Change'

During the Old City of Glasgow Police days when wages were poor, the cops relied on shops and companies giving a 'discount' to police officers.

We would also get the odd 'steak pie', 'six rolls', pint of milk or 'apple tart' handed in to the office from the various delivery van drivers.

Amalgamation came upon us and in 1975 and we were united with cops from the Paisley area, who were 'slightly' naïve as to these practices.

However, during a particular nightshift, a certain County Sergeant was partnering one of the 'Glasgow' cops.

About 0500 hours, early in the morning, the Glasgow cop was driving the patrol car, when he suddenly sped off along the road after a 'bread' van.

Once alongside it, he activated his 'blue' lights and signalled the van driver to pull over and stop.

He then informed the Sergeant to remain in the car while he spoke with the driver.

Having spoken to the driver, he then accompanied him to the back of the bread van and within a few moments, the cop returned to the police car carrying a loaf of bread, which he placed in the rear seat before driving off again.

A few minutes later, the Sergeant asked the cop,

"What was that all about"?

He then explained, you signal the van driver to pull into the side and stop. Then you go up to him and ask to buy a loaf of bread, the driver is so relieved to know that he is not being 'booked', he duly obliges.

You then offer him the money, (28 pence) to pay for the bread, which he refuses to accept, saying,

"It's only a loaf mate, I'll not miss one"!

You then thank him and leave with your loaf.

Intrigued by the action of his fellow officer, the Sergeant tells the cop, he would like to try it.

About fifteen minutes later, they drive along the road and see another 'bread' van.
They immediately spring into action and pull up alongside it, with the 'blue' lights flashing, they signal the driver to pull over and 'stop'.

As he pulls over, the Sergeant tells the cop to stay in the patrol car and let him try it out himself.

Up to the drivers window he goes and within seconds, he is walking with the driver to the back of the van.

They are out of view for a few moments, then the Sergeant appears in the rear view mirror, walking towards the police car, carrying.... Four loaves of bread!

He then opens the car door and places them in the rear passenger seat.
As he enters the Police car, the cop remarked,

"Four loaves Sarge, you're a bit greedy there"?

To which the Sergeant replied sheepishly,

"Not really,

He didn't have change of a (£1.00) pound"!!

'Signing Session'

In possession of an arrest warrant for Tommy Morrison, I called at his last home address.
Due to his record of violent behaviour towards the Police, three other officers accompanied me.

After checking with the nameplates of each tenant living in the tenement close, I made enquiries with a few of them as to his whereabouts, but to no avail. Not known at this address!

A few days later, I was working within the office, when two detective officers from the Scottish Crime Squad called with an enquiry in the area.

While in conversation with them, they informed me they had called at the house of Morrison and cited the same address as the one I possessed for Tommy.

Further talks revealed that we were both interested in the same person, but they had just come from his house, where they had obtained a written witness statement from him with regards to their enquiry.

I checked with them the address they had for him and it turned out, he was staying, 'care of', his girlfriend, with her name, 'Galvin' on the nameplate of the apartment door.

Whilst noting his statement, they had taken all his relevant particulars, including his home telephone number.
I called the number, which was answered by his girlfriend and told her I was one of the officers of the Scottish Crime Squad, who had called at her house to speak with Tommy and explained,

I had forgotten to have him sign his statement, could he possibly call within the next half hour at the local police office and do so.

The Police Officers of the Scottish Crime Squad, sat quietly looking on with interest, at my calling their witness with this excuse, but after a few minutes, they saw the funny side and couldn't contain themselves.
As they left the office, they insisted I call them and let them know the outcome.

Sure enough, within the half hour, the door of the police office opened and in walked Tommy Morrison.

"Hello mate, I'm here to sign a statement for the Scottish Crime Squad"! He said assuredly.

"Oh right, can you just confirm your name and date of birth for me please"? I asked him.

He quickly reeled off, "Thomas Morrison, date of birth, 25. 10. 1958"

"That's what it says here Tommy, you're the man I'm wanting"! I said.

I then walked around to the side door of the front office and opening it up I invited him inside.
As we entered the office area, I then led him through to the detention room, where I opened the door.

He confidently entered the Detention cell, totally unaware of where he was going.
Once safely inside, I locked the door behind him.

I then took great satisfaction in telling him,

"As 'Jeremy Beadle' would say, Tommy, You Have Been Framed"!

And all performed by yours truly, with the minimum of fuss!

'Make Me Go Faster'

My partner 'David Ball' and I went over to the Police Federation Office, so that David could purchase a pair of Police sunglasses, which they sold at a very competitive price.

In he went, while I waited outside.
I could see him, trying on several pairs, until he satisfied himself.

Out he came smiling like a Cheshire cat, wearing his new 'make me drive faster' sunglasses.
As he was about to get into the Police Land Rover, I asked him to adjust the 'wing mirror' on his side'.
Placing the sunglasses on his seat, he duly obliged, before jumping into the jeep, planting his big fat arse on top of his brand 'new' sunglasses 'breaking' them!!

'Road Accident Excuses'

'I had been shopping for plants all day and was on my way home. As I reached an intersection, a hedge sprang up, obscuring my vision and I did not see the other car'.

'I was on my way to the doctor with rear end trouble, when my universal joint gave way, causing me to have an unplanned accident'.

'Disposing of Evidence'

George Cowley was a cop from the East end of Glasgow, working out of the 'old' Tobago Street Police Office.

His 'pet hate' was the 'scrap metal men', the guys who went about the streets, uplifting old bits of cars, washing machines, copper piping, etc, anything that earned them some 'beer' money. George was always stopping them and checking out their vehicles looking for defects.

One particular day, George was just leaving the Police office, when he saw 'Tank' Irwin, the 'Del Trotter' of Bridgeton, coming down the street towards him, in his 'pick up' truck, fully laden with 'scrap metal'.

He stepped out into the middle of the road and signalled for 'Tank' to pull over to the side of the road and stop.

"Right Mr Irwin, let's just check your vehicle for any defects"!

Said George, as he then began to examine the vehicle for faults.

At this point, 'Tank', a likeable rogue, got out of his drivers seat and began to follow George around on his inspection of the vehicle.

"I don't think you'll find anything Mr Cowley, I've just put it through an M.O.T." Said a confident 'Tank'

"Well we'll see". Replied George, as he continued with his thorough examination.

Unable to detect any obvious faults, they both arrived back at the front of the vehicle.

George began lecturing 'Tank', prior to letting him go.

Just at that moment, George's eyes lit up,

"Got you"! He said ecstatically.

He then put his hand through the open window and removed the 'Road Tax' disc, which was being displayed on the pick-up windscreen and on examining it very carefully, he cried out,

"Ya beauty! I've got you! Fraudulent display of a Road Tax"!

George could hardly contain himself as he 'jigged' about the footpath in complete and total ecstasy.

Whilst engaged in his 'victory' celebration, 'Tank' remained very calm and collected. Then he said,

"Can I see it please Mr Cowley"!

Not thinking about the consequences of his actions, George handed the fraudulent Road Tax disc over to 'Tank', who without the slightest hesitation, promptly crumpled it up into a ball and stuffed it into his mouth.

As his evidence was being 'chewed' before his very eyes, George jumped onto the back of 'Tank' and placed his hands around his neck in an effort to try and prevent him from 'swallowing' his 'fraud' case evidence.

On seeing, what appeared, as an unprovoked physical attack by George on 'Tank', this prompted some of the other cops, who were coming out of the Police Office, to run over and pull George away from Tank and restrain him.

This was all the time 'Tank' required and with one final 'gulp', he had disposed of the entire evidence.

'The Ballad of Big Bad Alec'

Big Alec MacLellan was a gentle giant who was responsible for the running of the Police motor vehicle pound.

He was the guy you went to see about getting your car back, when it was towed away by the polis, because it ended up in his vehicle pound.

He was a 'character' in the Police and a 'legend' in his own mind. This poem was written to celebrate his retiral in 1982.

There was a big polis called Alec, custodier of the Police vehicle pound
When customers called at his office, they could never find Alec around

There would often appear a wee notice, which plainly in pencil did say
"I'll only be out for a minute", but he really meant 'all bloody day'

I suppose he's gone out to the pub, 'Maxwell's' or maybe 'McNee's'
It was heard from one of his colleagues, "he'll drink till he lands on his knees"

His last trip was out to the 'bookies', he walked from the 'Pound' in a dream
He ended up in the chemists, and asked them for 'vanishing cream'!

The End

'No Hiding Place'

In possession of an apprehension warrant, I called at the home address of the named accused and I knocked on his door. After a moment, his wife answered the door.

I made her aware of why I was there and she swore to me, hand on heart that Joe was not in the house and hadn't stayed there for some time.
She also stated, she was unaware of his present whereabouts.

I asked if I could make a customary search of the house, in order to satisfy myself and also to confirm her story.
She reluctantly agreed to my request.

Whilst engaged in my search of the house, which was also occupied by several of her children, all under the ages of five years old. I was about to leave, when the wife stopped me in the hallway and said, she would contact me immediately, should he return home.

At this point, my attention was drawn to one of the small children, standing in a bedroom.
I looked through the 'hinge' opening of the door.

To my surprise, she was facing a double wardrobe and saying,

"Dah"! "Dah"! ...."Dah"! "Dah"!

She was also holding her outstretched hands up toward the door.

I continued to watch her for a moment, when suddenly, a hand appeared from inside the wardrobe and began waving the child away.
The hand then disappeared back inside.

Desperately trying not to laugh, I entered the room, knocked on the wardrobe door and said,

"Knock, Knock, Dah! Dah! Guess who's here to see you"?

The accused fell out the wardrobe laughing uncontrollably and said,

"See weans! Don't ye just love them"?

'New Release'

I have just been informed the Strathclyde Police Pipe band are to release a new CD of 'Scotlands' finest bagpipe tunes.

The only hold up is, what to call it.

How about 'Criminal'?

'More New Releases'

Strathclyde Police Pipe band performed in a recent competition.

I'm informed they played a haunting melody.

'Haunting' because they were 'Murdering' it!
(Now their just jokes guys, you're not bad!)

'Credit Fraud'

An accused male appeared up in court for Credit Card fraud.
Having been found Guilty, he received a hefty fine from the Sheriff.

The Defence Agent turned to his client and asked him how he would like to pay.

To which he confidently replied, "American Express"!

'No Armchair Stampede'

There had been an incident, at the rear of 'Celtic' Football Park in Glasgow, whereby, it was alleged, the Strathclyde Police 'mounted' branch officers, had 'stampeded', on horse back, football supporters, who had congregated in the area of Janefield Street, Glasgow.

This sensitive enquiry was being dealt with by one of our most senior and respected officers, Chief Superintendent John T Dickson.

During this ongoing enquiry, there was an international football match coming up, between Scotland and England at Hampden Park and I was trying to get tickets for it.

This particular day, I was called into Superintendent Irwin's office and he said to me,

"I've to ask you Harry, are you still looking for tickets for the big game, if so, Mr Dickson has two for sale"?

Having replied that I was looking for tickets, he called Mr Dickson at his office in Pitt Steet HQ, to inform him.

"Right Harry"! Said the Superintendent. "You've to go up to his office right now"!

I immediately went straight to Police Headquarters and knocked on his office door.

"In you come, Harry"! He said, then he opened a drawer and taking out the match tickets, he handed them over to me.

"Now-a-days, I prefer to watch the game in the comfort of my armchair in the house"! He said convincingly.

To which I said, jokingly of course,

"Well, let's be honest sir, you've less chance of getting trampled by a big bloody Police horse"!

Needless to say, he was not amused by my comment!

But I bet he had a right good 'chuckle' after I left his office!

'A Clash of Personalities'

I was summoned to the Chief Inspectors office for my Appraisal / Assessment, commonly referred to as your M.O.T.
Halfway through the appraisal report, the Chief Inspector said,

"I detect from some of the remarks made by your Shift Sergeant, you don't get on with him"?

"I think that's a fair observation", I replied.

"What appears to be the problem"? He asked me.

"It's just a clash of personalities sir". I said.

"A Personality clash"? He enquired before continuing.

"Do you think a change of shift would help"?

Whereupon I replied with a straight face,

"Frankly, no sir!

I don't think he could get on with anybody"!

'Don't Blow a Fuse'

One day my partner 'O'Reilly' arrived at the Police Office, in his new car, a second hand 'Hillman Avenger'.

Proud as punch he was, as he led me on an inspection of it.
There was the statutory coloured dice hanging from the interior mirror, also, stuck on either side of the front windscreen was 'Eddie' and 'Mary', very impressive and the wee dog with the 'bobbing' head in the rear window passenger shelf. A classic!

On the dashboard, he had fitted an impressive array of about twelve coloured switches onto a 'velvet cloth material' switchboard extension, which protruded out from the original Hillman dashboard.

He could not contain his obvious enthusiasm as he gave me a demonstration of the 'Changes' he had made, with the adding of the extra switches and their operational functions.

"This one operates new 'fog' lights at the front and this one, operates new lights at the rear"!

He continued. "This one is high intensity lights I've fitted and this switch here operates a quadraphonic stereo music system"!
He then 'flicked' the switch down and out 'blasted' a 'David Bowie' song.

"And this one"...

At this point, I interrupted him, as smoke began bellowing out from behind his new 'switch' dashboard.

"I take it this one operates a getaway 'smokescreen' or is it a direct line to the local 'Fire Brigade' Station?

O'Reilly looked on in disbelief,

"Shit"! "The wiring system's faulty"! He replied, frantically panicking.

"Quick Harry, get a fire extinguisher"!

"What switch should I press for that then"? I asked facetiously, while trying to remain calm.

Within 'Five Minutes', O'Reilly's 'Pride and Joy', was reduced to, 'Ashes to Ashes'!!

And O'Reilly was left 'Aladdin Sane'!!

'Religious Exams'

During the 'Traffic Advanced Driving' exam at Tulliallan Police College.
My colleague, 'Willie Smith' was filling out the questionnaire attached to his exam paper, with his Name, Divisional Number, Registered Number, Etc.

Just below this, it asked for you to write down your 'Region' and Willie, having misread it, wrote down 'Protestant'!
Much to the amusement of the Instructors and his fellow students.

'Lucky Me'

During an 'Old Firm' football match in Glasgow, a drunken fan was shouting and gesticulating abuse at my colleague and I.

When we went towards him, he ran off across the busy Main Road without looking and was promptly 'blootered' by a bus.
As I went to his assistance, he looked up at me, unfazed and said,

"Wiz a no' lucky I didnay hurt myself 'there"?

"Not really son"! I replied, as we jailed him!

'I Never Parked It Like That'

Colin Muir was a very laid back cop, whom I worked with for a short time as a young probationer.
His 'nickname' amongst the local 'neds' was 'Gallus', due to his laid back attitude and the way he reacted when dealing with them. He also 'loved' himself to bits and fancied himself as a charmer.

This particular night, we received a call to attend at the 'Pollokshaws Burgh Halls' due to a disturbance at a 'Wedding' reception, caused by local 'gatecrashers'!

On our arrival, we parked and locked, the Police 'panda', outside the main door and entered the hall, to deal with the complaint.
There was a large crowd in the hallway who dispersed 'sharpish', on seeing us, as we entered the main reception hall.

"Right, what's the problem, my man"? Gallus enquired from one of the guests.

That was the signal for the entire wedding party to try and all speak at the one time.

"Woh, woh, woh, cool the beans"! "Now, what about you sweetheart, can you tell me what happened"!

Said 'Gallus' as he pointed to a rather pretty young female, taking hold of her arm and leading her to one side.

During the following conversation that took place, 'Gallus' spent more time, 'chatting up' his hand picked 'reporter', noting her name, address and telephone number.

While this was taking place, the elderly male 'Hall Keeper', tried several times to interrupt 'Gallus', while he was in full flow, but 'Gallus' would repeatedly, tell him not to interrupt and wait his turn.

Finally, 'Gallus' walked over to the stage and interrupted the Wedding 'Band', right in the middle of them performing, 'You're the one that I want'!
Taking the microphone off the singer.

All the time, I stood there being the 'boy', quietly 'cringing' with embarrassment, at the unbelievable way he was dealing with this complaint.

He then assured the entire wedding 'party', over the 'microphone', that he was the local 'Sheriff' and this was his area and all the 'neds' feared him.
Now that he had made a personal appearance at the wedding reception, they would be too 'frightened' to return, because, more than anything, they wouldn't want to upset him.
He finished off like the 'Master of Ceremony' for the function, by announcing,

"I want you all to enjoy the rest of your night, especially, John and Morag, the happy couple".

He then led the Wedding Party with a 'toast' to the 'Happy Couple', before handing the microphone back to the band singer.

I couldn't believe it, when the Wedding Party, table after table, stood up and 'applauded' him.
Some of the guests even held out their hands to shake his and a few of the ladies even kissed him, as he left the hall waving them goodbye.

Out in the hallway, the elderly 'Hall Keeper' was still waiting to speak with him.

"Right my man, what's your problem then"? Said a confident Gallus.

The old Hall Keeper said,

"I don't have one sir, but I think you do! Look"!

He then ushered us to the main door entrance of the Hall.

Where, to the total embarrassment and humiliation of 'Gallus' and I must admit, the complete and total amusement of the Old Hall Keeper and myself, the 'neds' who gatecrashed the wedding had, on their way out, overturned our Police 'panda' car and rolled it over onto it's roof.

'The Music of Life'

The police were attending a call regarding a suicide report of a male within a tenement building.

Whilst there, awaiting the arrival of the Casualty Surgeon and staff from the City Mortuary, a female neighbour appeared at her door and enquired,

"What's the matter Constable"?

"It's your neighbour hen, he's committed suicide"! Replied the Officer.

The shocked female 'gasped' in horror.

"How did he do it"? She asked, concerned.

"He hung himself last night"! Responded the Officer.

The female paused for a moment, before turning around to her son, who was standing just inside the door and saying,

"Here! I hope you weren't playing that bloody Bob Dylan"!

'Ladies and Gentlemen, Ben Doon'

Whilst a member of the Police Social Committee, it was your duty from time to time, to act as the Master of Ceremony for the night at a cabaret function.

Up until now, I had always managed to avoid it, but, with the absence of some of the members, I was nominated to take my turn.

The star of the Cabaret was a very funny comedian, called 'Ben Gunn', whom I was introduced to on his arrival at the club earlier on in the evening.
He gave me this 'spiel' that he wanted me to use in my introduction of him, about having just returned from a very successful tour of America and was now appearing as top of the bill, on the Sidney Devine Silver Jubilee Show, being held at the Pavillion Theatre, in Glasgow.

"After the performance", he said, "We'll have a drink"!

Now, earlier on that evening, this would not have been a problem, however, after several large whiskies, the art of 'breathing' for me was becoming a big problem.

It came to the penultimate act, a 'Caribbean Steel Band', dressed in bright Orange shirts. They looked like they had all been 'Tangoed' as they played their big oil drums.

By the way, the nearest they came to the 'Caribbean', was in a 'brochure', I new three out of the four of them personally, having recognised them as drivers on the Corporation buses, working out of the Larkfield Bus Garage in Glasgow.

With the previous act, a Country and Western act called 'The Pheasant Pluckers', I had developed dyslexia and read their introduction wrong referring to them, as some 'C.... with Vests on', 'The Pleasant F......'.

The other Committee Members were telling me, "Right Harry, we think you got away with that one", but not to make any mistakes with the introduction of 'Ben'!

I jumped onto the stage with my 'microphone' and said confidently,

'Let's hear you one more time, all the way from 'Jamaica' (Street), 'The Caribbean Steel Band'!
The assembled audience applauded enthusiastically.

As the applause died down, I said,

"They rejected an engagement to go on a Worldwide Tour! Apparently two of the band members wanted to go somewhere else"!

"I'm also informed that the boys want me to tell you, they're sorry there will be no encores, as there's a shortage of bus drivers tonight and they've all got to report for double shifts"!

I continued in this vein, getting carried away with myself, leaning on the microphone stand.

"Two of the band are actual twins"! "They used to be triplets but they ate the other brother between them one night! In true conundrum fashion, he was ate before he was seven"!

"Now! We have come to the star of our show. An act that has been thrown off more stages than big John Wayne"!

"Infact, he tell's me, he is just back from America, where he underwent a 'nose' transplant, but unfortunately, his finger rejected it"!

Suddenly, through the 'smokey haze', I could see some of the Committee members making their way down the sides of the hall, trying not to draw too much attention to themselves, but I was on a 'roll' and wasn't going to get off the stage that easily, so I continued,

"He was telling me earlier that while he was in America for three weeks, he lost 9 stones of ugly fat ...

Apparently he got a quickie divorce"!

That was the last straw, one of the Committee had the other end of the 'microphone' and was pulling and tugging it, so in order to prevent any further embarrassment, I quickly announced,

"So will you please put your hands together and give a big 'Lochinch' Police Club welcome to the one and only Mr Ben 'Doon'!! Hic!

Ben was not one bit amused at my introduction. He took the 'mike' off me and called me a frustrated comedian.
He then cut his cabaret act short by twenty minutes and left the club.

Needless to say, I was never again asked to perform as the 'Master of Ceremony' at a Police Social Club!!
Although I did apologise to Ben when we met on another occasion! I think he still carried a grudge!

'Hearing Things'

A 'Ned' in the Court was being sentenced for his offence.

"Have you anything you would like to say"? Asked the Sheriff.

The Accused replied rather despondently, "Fuck all"!

The Sheriff called out to the Procurator Fiscal, "What did he say there"?

"Fuck all! M'lord"! Replied the Fiscal.

To which the Sheriff said, "I'm sure I heard him say something"!

'Harry the Unknown 'Osmond'

I shall now reveal a hidden talent and long time 'secret'.

Back in the early seventies, the 'Apollo Theatre' in Glasgow, was a very popular venue, for all big music acts, 'Status Quo, Thin Lizzie, 'Dr Hook, 'The Osmonds'…

During this time, I had the good fortune to be working at the 'Osmond' brothers concerts. I was also quite friendly with 'Jan', the manager of the 'Apollo' at that time.

Whilst on duty, I was speaking with 'Jan' and asked him if he could get me a souvenir or autograph from the band for my young sister 'Kim', who was about twelve years old and a really big fan. 'Jan' said he would see what he could do for me.

A short time later, 'Jan' called me over and said he had managed to secure, an autographed L.P. Album called 'The Plan' for Kim, which he would keep in his office and give me after the concert.

I was 'over the moon', I couldn't contain my excitement and called my mother to let my young sister know what I had secured for her.

After the 'Osmonds' and the 'screaming' teenage girl audience had all but gone, I went to Jan's office to collect my prized possession.

To my complete and utter disappointment, Jan informed me that during the concert, a thief entered his office and had stolen various items, the autographed 'Plan' album being included.

I was devastated at this news.

What was I going to do? I had promised my little sister an autographed 'Osmond' album.

Fortunately, Jan came to the rescue, with another 'Osmond' album, minus the autographs of one of the biggest and most popular bands in the world.

What was I going to do again? Simple! I signed all the autographs of, 'Donny', 'Merryl', and 'Jay'!
The rest of the Osmond brothers..., well that was my colleagues accompanying me on the night.

I'll spare the blushes of who were little 'Jimmy' and 'Marie'!

So Kim, having treasured the 'Plan' for all these years, the secret's out...

Kim, your big brother Harry was, 'Donny Osmond'! "And they called it puppy lov"...... 'Shuttt Uppp'! "Oops, sorry pet"!

'Guess Who'?

Imagine working for a Company with slightly more than 500 employees and has the following statistics;

29 have been accused of spousal abuse, 7 have been arrested for fraud, 19 have been accused of writing bad cheques, 119 have directly or indirectly bankrupted at least 3 businesses, 3 have been sentenced for assault, 70 have been refused Credit Cards due to bad debt, 14 have been arrested on drugs related charges, 8 have been locked up for theft by shoplifting, 20 are currently defendants in Criminal lawsuits and in the last year, 83 have been arrested for drunk driving.

Can you guess who the Organisation is?

It's the 535 members of the United States Congress!
The same people who introduce hundreds of new laws each year.
It makes you wonder how the British Government would fair?

'Bombs Away'

In the late seventies, early eighties, we were receiving numerous 'Bomb Alerts', all false alarms, except, for a particular night I received a call to attend, a well-known 'Irish' pub, in the Gorbals area of Glasgow.

While en-route, I received another call, confirming it as a genuine 'Bomb' gone off!

Within several minutes, I had arrived to find the entire area, 'swamped' with Police personnel. No one was seriously injured.

I left after a short time and was instructed to return to my office and see the patrol Inspector.

Now, his 'nickname' was 'the Olympic Flame', because, he never went out!

He wanted fully appraised, as to what had happened?

To which I said, with a straight face,

"Right, allegedly, a man wearing a 'Rangers' scarf, entered the pub and walked up to the barman and asked for three bottles of 'Bells' whisky, four bottles of 'Smirnoff' vodka, three bottles of 'Gordons' gin, two dozen cans of Tennents lager, two dozen cans of McEwans pale ale and four dozen cans of McEwans export, then, at this point, the barman interrupted him and said,

"This is going to cost you a bomb"!

The man, took an object out of his jacket, threw it towards the barman and said, "There you are, you have two minutes"!

The 'Flame', looked puzzled, laughed nervously, then said,

"Is that true"?

'To Hell with Tulliallan'

While attending at the 'Tulliallan' Police College, Stirling, for my three month probationer training spell, I was taking part in a football tournament being held.

Several teams were made up from the large contingent of probationer students.

The team I was in, had qualified for the next round and I was supporting my 'mate', Jimmy Clark, playing for his team, in hope that he would also qualify for the next round.

Unbeknown to me, also present as a spectator at the rear of the hall was none other than the Director of Junior Training, or D.J.T. as he was better known and Inspector John Elliot, Head of the Junior Training Instructors.

Anyway, during the game being played, Jimmy had the ball at his feet, beat two defenders and with only the goalkeeper in front of him, he knocked the ball wide of the post.

"Jesus Christ"! I shouted out in sheer frustration.

At this 'blasphemous' outburst, the D.J.T. Asked Inspector Elliot,

"Who said that"?

The Inspector shouted at me, "Was that you Morris"?

"Yes sir"! I replied, annoyed at myself for shouting out.

"You'll go to hell for that, Morris"! He said.

To which I responded in a jocular manner by replying,

"With all due respect sir, I've been here for two months and three weeks"!
Raising a laugh from the many students present.

Later the same day, I was called up to the D.J.T.s office and disciplined for my spontaneous remarks.

How trivial!!

'Funny Text from a Friend'

My missus came out of the 'shower' one morning and stood naked in front of the bedroom mirror and said to me,

"My eyes are baggy, my tits are sagging and I look horribly fat and ugly, pay me a compliment darling"!

To which I replied,

"Okay, your eyesight's 'fucken' spot on"!

'Grass is Grass'

A professional footballer was arrested for possession of 'cannabis'.
The young arresting cop, on recognising him, asked,

"What's the best, 'grass' or 'Astroturf'?

The footballer replied sarcastically,

"I don't know, I've never 'smoked' Astroturf"!

'Anti Abortion Demo'

I was on duty at a large public 'demonstration', (yes another demonstration in Glasgow).
This time it was being held by a group of 'Anti Abortionist'!

It was a beautiful bright 'sunny' day in Glasgow and they were marching all the way on foot from 'Blythswood Square' to the 'Glasgow Green', in the east end of Glasgow.
My attention was drawn to the 2,500 or so demonstrators and how I could divide them up into five sections, of which were the following;

'One fifth of the demonstrators being men! C'mon guys?

'The second fifth was made up of children and most of them, had an awful lot of growing up to do, before they needed to worry about abortions'.

'My third section was made up of nuns! I'm saying absolutely nothing, because I respect their total commitment to the church'.

'The fourth section was made up of old age pensioners.
Now let's face it, there's virtually no chance, unless you're Sophia Loren, of ever getting pregnant at their age, so what have they got to be worried about'?

'Which brings me to my last section.
This was made up of many heavily pregnant' mothers to be' and most of them, by the end of the 'Demonstration' march, were so exhausted and totally exasperated with the heat, coupled with the constant 'greeting', 'moaning' and 'complaining' of their own children and those belonging to the other demonstrators, to the extent, that by the time they arrived at the finish'.

Several had already changed their opinions and were now definitely all 'for' it.

The following week, there was a 'Pro Abortion Demonstration' and I'm positive I recognised a few familiar faces!

'What Are You Doing?'

I called at the local Police Office and entered the 'Radio Control Room' and asked the female civilian computer operator, to check a car registration number, of a suspect 'stolen' vehicle.
The female assistant was about to drink a cup of coffee at the time, but agreed to my request.
While she was entering the details of the car, I lit up a cigarette and hovered around the back of her, leaning over her shoulder, as she made my vehicle check.
Whilst leaning over her, viewing the computer screen, I saw out of the side of my eye, what appeared to be a round ashtray, to my right hand side.

Still viewing the computer screen, I put my hand over and began to 'stub' out my cigarette 'butt'!
After three or four attempts, to put my cigarette out, I looked over towards the ashtray and to my horror, I discovered, what I thought was a cigarette ashtray, turned out to be her 'Wagon Wheel' chocolate biscuit!
I frantically, I began to try and discretely wipe off the cigarette ash and return the biscuit to it's original appearance and appetising best, but, while in the process of doing so, the female computer operator, slowly turned around and caught me in the act.

Over the years that followed, I presented her with numerous packets of biscuits, but I don't think she ever forgave me for her what I did with her 'Smokey Wagon Wheel'!
Mind you, I just might have created a new 'Wagon Wheel' flavour!

Bye the way Cathy, I also stopped smoking shortly after this!

'The Court Jester'

I was working at the High Court in Glasgow, along with several other cops, as part of the Courts Branch.

Whilst I was sitting within the 'Police Control Room', with 'Wee Hughie Dewar', the cop who operated the 'security gates' and 'cameras'.
I was going through some of my voice impersonations with Hughie and we were having a good laugh.

At this point, five out of the six courts, were finished for the day and the cops who were working in them, were all sitting about the Police 'Common room' (lounge), quietly reading a newspaper or playing cards to kill time, until they received permission to go home.
This was the normal practice and I found it extremely 'boring', sitting about, so Hughie had suggested I telephone the Duty Officer, whose room was directly opposite our position and who was responsible for the Police Officers employed within the courts.

I would then impersonate the 'Courts Branch' Inspector and we would observe his reaction, from the window of our room.
I rang his telephone and watched as he answered it, I then said,

"Hello Paul", "Inspector Harrison here, has anybody been looking for me"?

"Yes sir"! Paul replied. "Mr Martin was looking for you"!

"Okay, I'll give him a call"! I said. "What's happening elsewhere with the courts then"? I asked him, aware that all but one of the courts was finished for the day.

"All my courts are finished for the day, bar one"! He replied immediately.

"Are the cops all sitting about in the 'Common room' then"? I enquired.

"Yes sir", "Do you want me to give them something to do here, or should I send them all over to the 'Sheriff Court to work"? Asked Paul.

"No, don't bother, just send them all home, they've worked hard today and deserve a break"! I replied rather convincingly.

"Okay sir, you're the boss"! He said reassuringly.

I then put the phone down and Hughie and I had a right good laugh at Paul's expense.
Suddenly, my facial expression changed, as I looked up along the 'cell' passage corridor and saw all the cops from the 'Common room', with their civilian jackets on and carrying their bags, coming towards me.
I quickly ran into Paul's room and informed him, it wasn't the Inspector calling, it was me doing an impersonation of him.

To which he said,

"Well, Harry boy, you better do another one and explain to this lot coming down the corridor, I don't think they'll be happy with you"!

I then, ran out to meet with them and casually putting my hands up, I said,

"Sorry guys, you've got to go back to the common room, Paul was just 'winding' you all up.
He's sitting in his office laughing, the 'lousy' bugger"!

This news was greeted by groans from the disgruntled, cops, who were very annoyed with Paul for his 'sick joke'.

I managed, in my own imitable way, to avert the situation and 'pass the buck' on to Paul at the same time!

'Relief, for My Relief'

At the end of my shift, I was attending at a friends house to view a 'Live' boxing match and had arranged with another good friend of mine, also going, to call at the Police Office at the end of my shift and we could share a taxi together.
Now, my friend 'Brad', is a 'six feet' plus, black guy, who is also a 'deaf mute'!

Anyway, he duly arrived in my front office at the agreed time and I informed him using 'Sign Language' that I was just waiting for my 'relief' Station officer arriving, then we could go, but, in the meantime, to wait in the front office area!

Brad decided to view the various 'posters' of information, on the walls and after several minutes, the front door to the office opened.
Brad immediately 'felt' the draught from the door on his face and turned around to face it, as in walked 'Donnie', my relief officer.
With Donnie looking at me and Brad with his back to me, looking at Donnie, I spoke in a loud voice and said,

"For the last time sir, there is no one working here called 'Donnie' and he certainly hasn't been 'sleeping' with your wife, or daughter, now will you 'bugger' off out of the Police Office"!

All the time I was talking, Brad was staring at Donnie, who had 'froze' in his tracks and was staring back at Brad, with what can only be described as a 'startled' look, on his face and a distinct lack of colour.

Everything paused for a moment while Donnie suffered in silence, then I allowed a huge grin to cover my face and said,

"Don't look so worried Donnie, I'm only joking, he can't hear a word, he's totally deaf"!

At which point, Donnie gave a huge sigh of relief, before 'scurrying' off to the 'toilet' to 'relieve' himself! No doubt!

'The Spark-le is Still There'

After twenty five years of marriage, a Police Inspector returned with his wife to the hotel, where they had spent their first 'honeymoon' night.
The following day, the Inspector then drove her to an area, near a 'farmers field', where they had enjoyed their first romantic 'kiss'!

They both got out of the car and 'hand in hand', they walked over to the 'special spot'.
He took her in his arms and leaned her against the fence as he kissed her ever so passionately.

The wife suddenly responded in an 'erotic' manner, digging her nails into his back, gripping him tightly and biting his face, she then jumped up onto him and wrapped her legs tightly around his waist, squeezing him as she yelled and squealed ecstatically.

The Inspectors' reaction was one of sexual excitement,

"Darling, you weren't as amorous or vigorous as this twenty five years ago"!

The wife responded, by saying,

"No, and the 'farmers fence' wasn't 'electrified' then either"!!

'<u>The Demolition Man</u>'

One evening I received a call from my 'faither' in the Polis, 'Willie Craig', the Duty Officer of the 'Force Control Room'.
Willie wanted me to assist a distressed female, who was locked out of her house and calling from a nearby telephone kiosk.

I attended immediately and after comforting the upset female, she then explained that she had been out with her husband and another couple, for a meal and a drink.
During the evening, her husband complained of feeling unwell and decided to go home early, leaving her and the other couple, to enjoy the rest of the night.
On arriving home later, she was unable to gain access to her house, because of her husband's house key, still within the lock inside.

She stated, she 'knocked' on the door for a while, then she had tried phoning the house for almost thirty minutes, but there was no answer and she was now becoming increasingly concerned about her husband and his health.

The distressed female then directed me to her apartment door, which was on the first floor of a red sandstone tenement building.
The exterior house door was solid and had been decorated with mahogany 'wood grain' panelled plywood.
The fitted door 'facing', was of a fancy 'ogee' design and was finished off, with imitation wrought iron hinges, door knocker, letterbox, name plate and door handle.

All very nice and decorative.

Above the door, was a large colourful, stained glass window.

Having tried initially to force the door, with the minimum 'body' pressure, it called for more force to be used......the 'Doc Marten Boot'!

I had several attempts at kicking the door, but, to no avail, all I succeeded in doing was to 'burst' the decorative mahogany paneling on the door even more.
I also, due to the extreme force I was using, managed to 'crack' the mirrored background on the imitation 'gold' nameplate.
I made my apologies for the damage, to the 'sobbing' female, who waived them away, being more concerned with her husband and his state of health.

Change of plan!

I then tried, with the use of a large 'screwdriver', to remove the fancy 'ogee' door facing, in order to gain access to the door lock.
All was going well, until halfway down the facing.... 'Snap'!
The facing broke off.

I turned around to look at the female, standing, watching, with a paper tissue in her face, drying her sobbing tears, as I systematically demolished her door in installments.

"Oh just carry on and get me in"! She said.

I then proceeded to 'rip' the rest of the facing off the door and with the aid of the large 'screwdriver', I 'chipped' away at the door 'standard, to try and expose the 'mortice' lock.

'With no luck here'! I returned to 'kicking' the now, almost 'demolished' and unrecognisable, fancy decorative door.

With all the noise coming from my eager attempts to gain entry, the neighbour, opposite, from across the landing opened his door and on seeing the 'plight' I was facing, suggested,

"Why don't you just smash the window above the door and gain entry that way"?

At which point, our 'sobbing' female, still breaking her heart, shrieked at him.

"Why don't you just 'fuck off', don't you think he's done enough bloody damage to my door"?

Then realising what she had said in her outburst, she looked around at me and said,

"Oh, I'm sorry Officer, I know you mean well"!

She had just finished her apology when 'click'!

We all turned around as the door was opened and a very 'sleepy' looking male was standing there, dressed in vest and pants.

"What's all the racket"? He asked, completely unaware of all that had occurred.

The 'sobbing' female's facial expression changed as she charged at her husband, whom she had been so extremely worried about. She began to scream hysterically at him.

"You bastard, look what you've caused and there's nothing up wi' you"!

She then began to 'punch' and 'kick' him, as he tried to make his way along the entrance 'hallway', out of her reach.

As for me!

I didn't wait for her to thank me, I got off my mark quickly, before she had another look at her door and took revenge on me!

The result of the call to the Force Control Room was,

"Entry gained by the Police. All in order. The female reporter wishes to thank the Police for a job well done"!

Then I added, "And did we know the number of a good joiner"!

'The Glasgow Olympics'

A few years ago, whilst watching athletics on the television and being privileged to see the intense methods of preparation, undertaken by some of the worlds most notable athletes, it suddenly struck me, the amount of preparation, the every day wee Glasgow 'punter' put into his, by that, I mean his '100 metres' and '200 metres' Sprint Race, his 'High Jump', 'Pole Vault' and 'Long Jump', etc…

You see, none of his athletical exploits are performed in such prestigious competition, but rather the opposite, …for example, When the situation presented itself and if you resided in a Glasgow tenement-housing scheme, the situation, would present itself regularly.

One minute, you would be playing in a tough competitive game of 'Rounders', 'Street Football' or 'Kick the Can', when all of a sudden….. 'Bang'!!
You looked up and the 'Polis' would be 'plodding' it out, coming down the street towards you.

'Whoosh'!! You were off and I mean off, your legs were just a 'blur', as they propelled you along at 'break neck speed'.

(That's very, very, fast, bye the way).

I hurdled every obstacle that came my way whether it was a 7' feet Garden Fence, an 8' feet Boundary Wall, or a 12' feet Opening over a Stream and any obstacle that I couldn't master, I would run straight through.

Wood and brick 'debris' would be brushed aside by my sheer speed and determination.

Linford Christie would have no chance. Nobody, but nobody was going to catch me!

Then suddenly, a strange but alarming thought struck me!

What the hell am I running for?

I'm the **Community Police** for the area!

'Learn to Drive'

One day while driving a traffic patrol car along the road, a black hackney carriage, (that's a taxi to you) suddenly and without warning, made a 'U' turn manouvere, in the roadway in front of my Police car, causing me to take evasive action to avoid a collision.

As I came to a stop, I leaned out of the drivers window of the Police vehicle and shouted at him,

"Where the hell did you learn to drive"?

To which the 'taxi' driver shouted back,

"With the polis, I used to be a traffic cop, with you Harry, remember"?

As it was, I then recognised him and sure enough, it was David Colvin an ex-Traffic cop!

'Speed Camera Excuse'

'I was suffering from a heavy cold and sneezed excessively, causing a chain reaction, whereby my foot pushed down harder on my accelerator causing me to speed at the wrong time'.

"THE ADVENTURES OF PC ARCHIE BAULD"

BY 'SEAMOR TOONS'

'Parking Disability'

There was a C.I.D. Officer nicknamed 'Sven' because of his 'Scandanavian' looks, tanned skin and physical build.
Apart from his smart stylish suits and blonde hair, he drove about in a white coloured sports type car, which suited his personality and stood out.

One day he went shopping with his present girlfriend at the time, to the newly opened 'Parkhead Forge Shopping Centre'. Unable to find a car Parking space near to the entrance door, Sven decided to park his fancy new sports car, in the only space available, a vacant 'Disabled Parking Space'.
Off they both went, hand in hand, turning his head back one more time, to view his shining pride and joy, parked safely in the car park.

After spending several hours going from shop to shop and accumulating bag after bag of groceries and clothing, it was time to leave the Centre and return to the 'Sven mobile'.

As they both strolled along the 'Mall' laden down with carrier bags heading for the exit doors, leading them to the car park.
Sven's infectious boyish smile on his face changed to one of shock, as he looked over and to his horror, saw his 'Dream Machine' being lifted by a 'Hiab' recovery vehicle, onto the rear of it, for removal.
Also, standing alongside taking notes, were two 'leather clad' Motorcycle Cops.

Quickly, Sven dropped his heavy grocery bags on the footpath and said to the girlfriend,

"Here, grab hold of that lot"!

Then, 'panic stricken', he ran up to the Motorcycle cops and enquired,

"What the hell are you doing, that's my car you're lifting"?

The motorcycle cop who was writing vigorously away in his notebook, paused for a moment, looked over at Sven and said,

"You're parked illegally in a 'Disabled Parking Bay' sir"!

Then checking Sven out visually, he added.

"And you certainly don't look disabled to me"!

Sven thought for a moment as he stared at the cop and turning around to view his girlfriend bringing up the rear, he turned back to the motorcycle cop and pointing over at her, he said confidently,

"Well does she look normal to you"?

They both looked over to see his slightly built girlfriend, laden down with all the heavy grocery bags, shuffling along in high heel shoes and struggling with great difficulty to carry them all.

The motorcycle cop allowed himself a wry smile before continuing with his notes.

As for the girlfriend, on hearing Sven's discourteous remarks about her physical condition, she dropped the grocery bags where she stood and shouted at Sven,

"Is that right ya big diddy"! "Well ye can just carry the messages yersel', I'm out of here"!

Before storming away in a bad mood.

A hard and expensive lesson for Sven to learn, but if you are not Disabled don't park in the Bay!

'0 --- 60 in Seconds'

During the miners strike and subsequent picket lines at Bilston Colliery, a young Police probationer was engaged in the picket line duty, whereby, the officers were 'pushed', jostled', 'spat upon' and struck by 'missiles' thrown at them.

The young Police probationer, finally snapped, unable to withstand it anymore, he broke 'ranks' and ran off screaming at the top of his voice,

"I can't take anymore! I can't take anymore"!

He ran as fast as he could, covering a distance of several hundred metres, when he eventually stumbled and fell over.
As he lay on the ground, with his head in his hands, sobbing uncontrollably, he heard a deep husky voice say,

"Get a grip of yourself lad"!

Looking over, in the direction of the voice, he saw a pair of highly polished black shoes.

"I'm so sorry Sergeant"! He blurted out.

The voice replied rather indignantly,

"Who are you calling Sergeant"? "I'm your Superintendent"!

To which the young probationer replied,

"Fuck me"! "Did I run that far"?

'I'd Know Her Anywhere'

A road accident occurred, resulting in a female passenger being fatally injured.

The driver of the vehicle, who was unconscious, had suffered serious head injuries, but, was identified by one of the police officers present, as David Green.

However, the problem arose, as to the identity of the female passenger.

On calling at David Green's relatives address to inform them of his injuries, they were informed he had a long-term relationship with Maggie Reid, who was separated from her husband.

Several enquiries later, they called at the home address of Robert Reid (husband) and made him aware of the road accident and their suspicions, that the fatally injured female could be his wife Maggie.

The husband was distraught at this news and sat down breaking his heart, as tears poured from his eyes.

One of the officers present, (Big Davie) gave him a glass of water and a cigarette, which he readily accepted, even though, he was later to admit, he had stopped smoking three weeks ago.

The next task was to convey the distraught Mr Reid, (several cigarettes later), to the City Mortuary, in Glasgow, in order to identify the deceased female.

At the mortuary, the officers displayed their sensitive side to Mr Reid and his loss.

They informed him, one side of her face had been badly injured and therefore, if he wished to, he could view the deceased, on the mortuary video display.
Mr Reid declined their offer, stating he would rather see her up close himself.

As he entered the room, he broke down again, prompting a 'flood' of tears.

"That's her, it's her, oh my God, whit will I tell the weans? She's gone! Their mammy's gone forever. Oh God, I miss her already"!

Deeply distressed, Big Davie led Mr Reid back to the Police car and returned him home to the comfort of his friends and family.

After noting the relevant particulars for his police report, Big Davie and his partner, several hours later, returned back to the police office.

As they entered the office, I said,

"What kept you two then"?

Big Davie replied,

"What kept us"? "We've been here, there and every 'bloody' where, trying to get the deceased female identified"!

"And did you get her identified"? I enquired.

"Eventually", said Davie. "It's Maggie Reid"!

"Maggie Reid"? I said, surprised. I then shook my head.

"Don't think so Davie". I replied.

"It was Harry"! Said Big Davie. "She's been identified"!

"Sorry guys, you're wrong, because Maggie Reid was in here only half an hour ago, asking, how badly injured David Green was and I might add, she looked very much alive and kicking"!
I responded.

Big Davie and his partner both looked at each other puzzledly! Before Davie then asked me,

"Well, who's in the City Mortuary, 'cause Robert Reid was positive, it was his missus lying there and he even identified her"?

"Well it wasn't his missus, it was 'lucky' Jackie Kelly's daughter, Sandra". I explained.

"The traffic cops have got the report, you must have just missed them at the City Mortuary"!

Big Davie 'slumped' down into an office chair.

"That bugger Robert Reid smoked about twelve of my 'fags', infact at one point, he was that upset, I was nearly greeting with him"!

His partner said,

"So much for his statement, I'd know her anywhere"! And what about the bit where he said,

"We had three lovely weans together. He must have been making love in the dark".

"Crikey, he even cuddled her body and kissed her"! Added Davie.

I then said,

"Well, he's in for a shock in the morning, when Maggie 'Knocks' on his front door"!

To which Big Davie retorted,

"Having seen his reaction tonight, he'll probably no' recognise her"!!

'Post it Thru' the Window'

'Stinker' Smith was the Police Officer in charge of the Temporary Police Office, which was a 'Portacabin', on Paisley Road, in Glasgow.

He was enjoying his favourite pastime, playing a game of cards during his 'refreshment break' period, along with some of the colleagues on his shift, when someone entered the front office.

Down went his 'cards' and through he went to the front part of the office to see who it was.
There, standing, holding an injured 'pigeon', was a small girl, who explained to 'Stinker', how she had found it on the roadway outside.

'Stinker' took possession of the injured pigeon and said he would contact the local 'Vet' to mend its obvious broken wing.
He then went into his drawer and handed the small girl a sweet, thanking her for her kindness.

'Stinker' returned with the pigeon, to the rear of the office, where the card game was taking place and opening a 'hopper' window, he promptly threw the pigeon out.
He then sat back down to play his hand of cards.

Several minutes later, the office door opened again as someone entered.

Down went his cards and through he went to see who it was this time.

To his surprise, the same small girl was standing there, this time holding a tiny 'kitten'!

"I found this little kitten outside on the footpath and I think it's lost its mummy"!

Reaching over to take possession of the kitten from her, he opened his drawer, handed her another sweet and said he would call the local 'cat and dog home', to come and collect it. He also suggested that she make her way home before her mummy reported her missing!

He then rushed through to the rear of the office and just as before, he opened the 'hopper' window and threw it out.
He then sat back down to play his hand of cards.

His colleagues made remarks about his lack of compassion, which he totally ignored.
Picking up his cards once again, he continued with his game, when.....

You've guessed it! The door to the front office was opened again. Becoming exasperated by these untimely interuptions to his card game, 'Stinker' slammed his cards down and said,

"If that's her again, I'm going to throw her out the window"!

He then rushed through to the front office, but to his surprise, it was a workman standing with the office door half opened and holding the reins of a 'horse pulling a cart'.

"Can I help you sir"? Enquired 'Stinker'.

"Yes you can mate"! Replied the workman. "I found this horse wandering about the roadway outside your office, with apparently no one in charge of it"! "It's going to cause an accident".

Before 'Stinker' could say a word, a voice called out from the rear of the office,

"Let's see you throw that out the window"!

Followed by some loud hysterical laughter!!

'The Lord Provost of Russia'

I had good fortune to meet and strike up a relationship with the late David Hodge, former Lord Provost of Glasgow.

This is a story he related to me about a visit he made to the former USSR.

My visit was full of surprises and I found so much that was completely different, to what I had been led to believe.

The people were happier than I expected.
It was interesting to attend church services and find 'standing room only'!

'I had a memorable experience in Sochi, a delightful resort on the Black Sea, with a tropical climate and unending sunshine.
Apparently, some years ago, a learned Professor experimented with citrus fruits and he found that all fruits of this family, could, by grafting, grow together on one single tree.

This actually happens in a 'Garden of Remembrance' and distinguished visitors and Russians of note are invited to graft, usually a fruit, native of their own country and these are labelled.

It was interesting to read the names of Uri Gargarin, Mrs Ghandi, Presidents and Ambassadors of most countries in the world, all represented within the 'Garden of Remembrance'.

I felt greatly honoured to be invited to humbly add the name of,

'The Right Honourable Lord Provost of Glasgow, David Hodge', to this impressive roll of honour.

It was quite unbelievable to see a tree bearing fruit, large and small, growing with oranges, limes, tangerines, lemons and grapefruit at one and the same time.

The Russians had this idea of living things growing together in a spirit of 'Peace and Friendship'.

Unfortunately,
The world has not yet, 'got the message' but, we must live in hope that one day, it will and people, not politicians, take over!

May I add, that as our climate does not encourage the growing of citrus fruits, therefore my graft was that of an orange, which originated from California.
It may take two years for a successful graft, to produce any ripe fruit, so maybe the football team, 'Moscow Dynamo' will one day be sucking on one of my oranges at half time, during a game.

'David Hodge, Former Lord Provost of Glasgow'.

'Reality Television'

If like me you are fed up to the back teeth with 'Reality Television' programmes, then let me put forward a suggestion, as a former Police Officer, of a 'Reality Television' show that would be worth the licence fee.

Now, my pet hate is that shite they call 'Big Brother' and the total 'diddies' they seem to audition for the show, who we, the paying public, are meant to watch, then phone up and vote for our favourite to remain in the household.
The eventual, 'Last Man Standing' so to speak, get's a few bob for surviving the 'Tiaras and Tantrums' of the many 'poofs', 'lebo's' and 'trannies'. And I'm not talking about a radio here!

My idea would be to fill the house as normal, then I would infiltrate the house with a 'Serial Killer' and let him 'do them in and whittle down the numbers. No telephone calls are needed.

Now that's a 'Big Brother Show' that would be worth watching!

'<u>Surprise! Surprise!</u>'

'Dougie Mack' was a cop with a mad passion for eating, 'pie and beans'. He adored them.
The only problem was, they didn't particularly agree with him.

You see, after consuming a few pints of Guinness and a few 'greasy' pies smothered in beans, he would suffer the most horrendous, obnoxious 'flatulence', infact, he was an out and out 'Pongo'!
Suffice to say, wherever he go, the 'Pongo'!

This did not unduly bother him, being a single bloke, until he met a policewoman and started dating her.
After dating regularly for over a year, the inevitable happened, when they got engaged and subsequently 'handcuffed', sorry, I mean married.
(Same thing)!

Several months later, Dougie was involved in a 'big drug bust' Court case and having obtained a conviction, he accompanied some of his fellow Drug Squad mates to a local 'hostelry' for a 'bevy' session to celebrate.

After swallowing numerous pints of Guinness, Dougie, the dutiful husband, made his excuses and left to catch his bus for home.
However, whilst standing at the bus stop awaiting it's arrival, he could smell an aroma, which had escaped his nostrils and taste buds for so long.......yes, it was 'pie and beans'!

The aroma to his nose, was, what 'Chanel' Number 5, is to a female....
'Pure nectar' from the gods.

As he stood there soaking up this 'bouquet of fragrance', he thought to himself, why not have just one?
One wouldn't hurt anybody and it would go a long way to satisfying his craving!

Finally convinced, he walked into the baker's shop and purchased one.
Oh how he enjoyed it, three bites and it was gone. Suddenly it came to him, it was still quite early, so why not have another and he could walk home, ridding himself of any foul flatulence on the way, thereby, he could arrive home to his house, with his lovely wife, non the wiser.

He talked himself into it and re –entered the shop.
The 'greedy pig' didn't stop at one and before he left the shop, he had scoffed three more. They hardly touched the sides of his throat, on their way down.

Off he went along the road, (wind assisted) striding it out like a 'Beat Policeman', 'farting' away, like a 'four bob rocket' at Guy Fawkes night, every few minutes, 'Bbbrrrpppp'!

It was like walking on 'Nike Air', without wearing the trainers, as each step he took, practically blew the backside out of his trousers. It was brilliant, with no one to bother about. He was only a threat to local wildlife.

Finally, almost at his house, he'd passed enough wind to re-write, 'The Wind in the Willows' and play the lead part of 'Pooh'.

He had contaminated the entire countryside with his foul waste and with time left for one more 'blow out' before he reached his front door.
He cocks his leg up to one side and…… 'Bbbrrrpppp'!

He then pauses for a moment, before 'minging' his doorbell. Sorry, ringing his doorbell!

After a few moments, his wife duly answers the door,

"Hello darling"! She said, as she leans forward placing a kiss on his cheek.

"Hello love", he responds, stepping inside the hallway, about to remove his jacket.

Then his wife says,

"Stop! Close your eyes darling, I have a nice surprise for you"!

Being the obedient husband, he complies with her request.
She then leads him along the hallway with his eyes tightly closed and into the lounge area of the house.

"Right", she says, "on the count of three, I want you to open your eyes"?

She begins to count, "one, two" and before she can say three, the house telephone rings.

"Stop"! "Don't open your eyes, promise me you'll keep them closed until I return", she pleads with him.

"I promise, I promise"! He replies.

On that note, his wife goes into the hallway to answer the telephone.

While awaiting her return, Dougie's stomach 'rumbles' with a build up of 'gas', which he has just got to be rid of...... Pronto!
He stretches his neck in the direction of his wife on the telephone and hearing her engaged in conversation, he let's rip....
'Bbbrrrpppp'!

What a 'rasper' this was and he doesn't even have a dog he can blame for it.

The smell is so strong you can practically taste it!

If it was 'canned' it could be sold as 'insect repellant'!

There's probably enough 'vitamins' in it, to 'cure' a 'Mediterranean' disease!

He begins blowing frantically and waving his hands about in an effort to disperse the 'pong' and still with his eyes closed tightly. What a good husband, (probably stinging anyway), he is totally minging!!

His wife calls out to him from the hallway.

"I hope you still have your eyes closed tightly"?

Dougie shouts back,

"Yes sweetie 'pie"!

There is nothing 'sweet' about this pie and he knows it, I can assure you!

"I wouldn't want to spoil your surprise for me".

He then quietly mutters to himself,

"I hope it's not pie and 'bloody' beans"?

He then 'giggles' to himself nervously.

Suddenly, he feels another rumble in his stomach, surely not again?
He feels like he is about to lift off!

'His 'bomb doors' are about to open fully'!

Is this a 'three minute' warning that the 'brownies' are coming?.... Definitely!!

However, he can't go to the toilet, because he would have to pass his wife in the hallway.
Panic stricken, he has a repeat of his last, 'fart', only double and in 'stereo',

'Bbrrrpppp – Bbrrrpppp'!! - 'Uugghhh'!!!

It feels as though, he has just passed a 'bowling ball'! Whole!

He is absolutely 'bowfin'!

He smells as if he is in the advanced stages of decomposing.

Local farmers would pay him, just to roll over and fertilise their fields.

The U.N. are searching Iraq for 'chemical weapons' and here we have our very own located in a Suburban Estate in Glasgow!

This last one takes the biscuit.

This time, the 'bunnet' is off his head and he is vigorously waving it about in front and behind him, in an effort to dilute the stench that he has produced, with the room's atmosphere.

Then panic, his wife finishes off her telephone conversation.

He stops his frantic waving and tries to act natural.

His wife enters the room and says,

"Right, did you open your eyes"?

"No darling, I did not", he replies. "Honest"!

"Good", says the wife, "Well, you can open them now"!

Very slowly, he opens his eyes and 'gasps' in horror!!

As seated around the room are police colleagues, friends and relatives, who in unison, burst into song,

"Happy Birthday to You"!!!   "Happy Birthday to You"!!!

'Aaaarrrrgggghhhhh'!!!

THE END

'LOOK OUT FOR, 'EVEN MORE LIES'! OUT SOON'.

MY APPRECIATION

THE AUTHOR WOULD LIKE TO THANK YOU FOR BUYING THIS BOOK AND HOPES THAT YOU HAD AS MUCH FUN READING IT, AS HE HAD WRITING, COLLATING AND COMPILING IT.

THE AUTHOR WOULD ALSO LIKE TO THANK THE MANY POLICE COLLEAGUES / CHARACTERS WHO MADE THIS POSSIBLE TO WRITE ABOUT, BUT IMPOSSIBLE TO TELL THE REAL TRUTH.

THE AUTHOR WOULD ALSO LIKE TO ADD, MOST OF THE NAMES HAVE BEEN CHANGED TO PROTECT THE 'GUILTY' AND MOST OF THE STORIES HAVE BEEN OVER EXAGERATED!

THE ADVENTURES OF P.C. ARCHIE BAULD CARTOONS BY 'SEAMOR TOONS' WAS CREATED AND WRITTEN BY HARRY MORRIS AND ILLUSTRATED BY DEREK SEAL.

HARRY MORRIS IS AVAILABLE AS AN 'AFTER DINNER' GUEST SPEAKER, FOR FUNCTIONS AND CAN BE CONTACTED VIA THE FOLLOWING E.MAIL ADDRESS ;

harry.morris51@virgin.net

OR

PO BOX 7031, GLASGOW, G44 3YN. SCOTLAND.

LOOK OUT FOR THE FOLLOW UP BOOKS IN THE
'TRILOGY'

'HARRY THE POLIS'

'EVEN MORE LIES' & 'NOTHING LIKE THE TRUTH'